# Holding the Center

America's Nonprofit Sector at a Crossroads

# Holding the Center

## America's Nonprofit Sector at a Crossroads

# Lester M. Salamon

A Report for The Nathan Cummings Foundation

Published by
The Nathan Cummings Foundation
1926 Broadway, Suite 600
New York, NY 10023

Library of Congress
    Cataloguing-in-Publication Data
Salamon, Lester M.
    Holding the Center: America's Nonprofit
    Sector at a Crossroads/
    Lester M. Salamon

    p. cm.
    Includes bibliographical references
    ISBN 1-886333-27-0
    1. Nonprofit organizations—United States.
2. Social service—Government policy. 3. Health.
I. Title

**The Nathan Cummings Foundation**
**1926 Broadway, Suite 600**
**New York, NY 10023**
**tel: 212.787.7300**
**fax: 212.787.7377**
**web site: www.ncf.org**

This publication was printed in January, 1997, on Trailblazer acid-free paper
produced from kenaf, a fast-growing fiber plant related to cotton and hibiscus.
Kenaf paper is produced in the U.S. without use of chlorine bleach or chlorine
gas, and—unlike the wood-pulping process in tree-based papermaking—there
is no release of dioxin by-products into the environment. For more information
on kenaf paper products, please contact Vision Paper, 505.294.0293

Designed by Bethany Johns Design
Printed by Herlin Press

*Things fall apart; the centre cannot hold.*

— W. B. Yeats, *The Second Coming*

# Contents

## List of Figures and Tables

### Figures

### Tables

## Preface

One of the great strengths of American society is the presence in this country of vigorous nonprofit organizations that provide a private means to pursue public purposes outside the confines of either the market or the state. Embraced within the nonprofit sector are some of our nation's premier universities and hospitals as well as thousands of community agencies that channel our impulses of charity, justice, and compassion to serve the common good and to support and empower those in greatest need. Most of the important social and political achievements of the past 50 years—from civil rights to women's rights to environmental protection—have originated in the passionate leadership and tireless efforts of nonprofit organizations.

For a variety of reasons, however, this important set of institutions faces serious challenges at the present time, challenges that could spell the end of the nonprofit sector as we know it. These challenges arise from many different quarters—cutbacks in government spending; proposed changes in tax policy; increased competition from for-profit organizations; a constricted view of legitimate charitable purposes; and lack of public understanding about what nonprofit organizations do and how they operate.

The purpose of this report is to identify and analyze these challenges and provide some suggestions about how they might be addressed. The report was prepared by Lester M. Salamon, a professor at Johns Hopkins University and a leading authority on this sector. Dr. Salamon's speech to the Annual Meeting of the Independent Sector in 1995 called attention to the serious crisis confronting America's nonprofit sector. In this report, commissioned by the Nathan Cummings Foundation, he extends and updates his analysis, sounding an alert for all who are committed to preserving and strengthening this vital component of our society.

The American nonprofit sector is at a critical crossroads. Fiscal pressures resulting from government budget cuts have forced many nonprofit organizations to increase their reliance on fees and service charges. In the process, for-profit firms have moved into their traditional areas of activity. Proposals for federal tax reforms could dramatically reduce the current incentives for philanthropic giving. Other proposed legislation would severely restrict the ability of nonprofits to serve as advocates—whether for public health measures, environmental protection, or services for the poor. Some state and local governments are also seeking to restrict the tax exempt status of nonprofit organizations.

The solution to the problems the nonprofit sector faces will not be found, Professor Salamon rightly notes, by trying to force the sector back to a mythical golden age of volunteerism and purely private charity. The modern nonprofit sector is complex and interconnected with both government and business in a host of complementary relationships. Rather than unraveling these relationships, we must find ways to make them work better.

At this time of realignment of government and corporate responsibilities, we cannot allow our great centers of learning, our places of spiritual practice, our theaters of creativity to decline. And we must strengthen the communities of caring—the diverse networks of people and organizations that provide critical services for the needy and work to shrink the vast gap between rich and poor.

In clear, well-documented terms, *Holding the Center* provides crucial information that is needed to make informed judgments about the future of the nonprofit sector. In disseminating this report, the Nathan Cummings Foundation hopes that policy makers and the concerned public will read the evidence and analysis presented by Dr. Salamon. We hope the report will help generate action to protect the nonprofit sector and strengthen its performance. Nothing less than the health of our democracy is at stake.

CHARLES HALPERN
President
The Nathan Cummings Foundation

## Foreword

This report seeks to "take the temperature" of America's nonprofit sector at what I believe is an especially crucial point in its development. More specifically, the report examines four important challenges that confront key segments of this sector at the present time and that raise fundamental questions about the sector's long-term character and health.

While an attempt is made here to analyze the status of the nonprofit sector and the challenges facing it as fully and fairly as possible, it must be acknowledged at the outset that this is a preliminary assessment at best. For one thing, key facets of both the pressures and the opportunities facing nonprofit organizations are poorly understood despite the significant growth of research in this field. For example, while few researchers would doubt that tax rates affect giving, there is considerable disagreement over the magnitude of these impacts as well as about their distribution among different types of organizations. Similarly, little is known about the forms and extent of the community benefits provided by nonprofit health care organizations and about how these benefits are being affected by the growing competitiveness of the health care market. Beyond this, however, limitations of time made it impossible to embrace within this report even all that is known. Crucial issues are therefore treated far less fully than I would like. Finally, an overview such as this invariably tends to emphasize problems and challenges and therefore fails to do justice to the rich variety of positive contributions that the many thousands of nonprofit organizations are making to national life. I therefore apologize to the millions of individuals working in these organizations for giving too little attention to the important difference they are making. My hope is that they will nevertheless see the value of the kind of diagnostic offered here as a way to get at least an early, preliminary warning on developments that could threaten their ability to continue making these contributions into the future.

I am grateful to Charles Halpern and Jennifer McCarthy of the Nathan Cummings Foundation for prompting me to prepare this report, and for providing the support and encouragement that made it possible; to Corrinne Schmidt and Catherine Carey of the Johns Hopkins Institute for Policy Studies for invaluable research assistance; to Bradford Grey, Charles Clotfelter, Richard Schmalbeck, Peter Goldberg, and Daniel Ritter for perceptive memoranda analyzing developments in their respective spheres of expertise; to Peter Berns, Elizabeth Boris, Virginia Hodgkinson, Reynold Levy, Michael O'Neil, Michael Seltzer, and Dennis Young for offering in the course of lengthy interviews their own perspectives on the issues facing the nonprofit sector; and to Claudine Brown, James Cummings, Ted Howard, Stanley Katz, Andrea Kydd, Amira Leiffer, Michael Lerner, Reynold Levy, Michael Seltzer, John Simon, and Edward Skloot for helpful comments on an earlier draft.

While I benefited greatly from this assistance, however, the responsibility for the findings and conclusions reported here is mine alone.

L. M. S.
Baltimore, Maryland
January 16, 1997

## Holding the Center:
## America's Nonprofit Sector at a Crossroads

LESTER M. SALAMON

1. The nonprofit sector is a crucial component of American life. It embraces major universities, symphonies, hospitals, and museums as well as thousands of local organizations, citizen advocacy groups, and grass-roots groups offering shelter and food to those in greatest need (pp. 5-9).

- Half of the hospital care, most of the human services, much of the higher education, a significant share of the low-income housing, and almost all of the symphonic music available in this country is provided by this set of institutions (p. 5);

- The nonprofit sector functions as a crucial support for our democratic political system and a mechanism to promote cherished national values of pluralism and individual initiative (pp. 7-9).

2. This important set of institutions confronts an extraordinary array of challenges at the present time, challenges that threaten the sector in harmful ways.

3. In the first place, the nonprofit sector faces a major *fiscal crisis* as a result of government budget cuts that threaten to disrupt an important partnership with government that was forged early in our country's history and that expanded greatly in the 1960s and 1970s (pp. 12-19).

- Because of this partnership, government budget cuts not only increase the need for nonprofit services; they also reduce the ability of nonprofit organizations to meet these needs.

- This is so because a considerable share of the revenues that nonprofit organizations rely on to finance their activities comes from government sources. In fact, government is the second largest source of nonprofit revenue, outdistancing private philanthropy by a factor of three to one (p. 14).

- Under the Congressional budget resolution passed in 1996, nonprofit organizations stand to lose a cumulative total of $90 billion, or 18 percent, of their federal support over the fiscal years 1997–2002. In some fields the reductions will be more severe: 25 percent in social services, 48 percent in international aid, and 51 percent in housing and community development (p. 18).

- These proposed new cuts come on top of steep reductions already enacted in the early 1980s that created fiscal difficulties for many types of nonprofit organizations and threatened many basic services.

4. It is highly unlikely that private giving will be able to offset these projected revenue losses.

- Just to offset the direct revenue losses that nonprofits face under the 1996 Congressional budget resolution—let alone the much larger overall reductions in federal spending in fields where nonprofits are active—the rate of growth in private giving would have to *triple* in FY 1997 and increase by up to 10 times its recent highs by the year 2002 (p. 21). Such growth is both unprecedented and unlikely.

- In fact, during the 1980s the growth of private giving *lagged behind* the growth of personal income. Far from filling in for the government budget cuts of the early 1980s, private giving actually fell as a share of nonprofit revenue—from 15 percent in 1982 down to 11 percent in 1992 (p. 23).

- Recent major tax overhaul proposals, such as the "flat tax" or the "national sales tax," would exacerbate this situation by shifting from income to consumption as the basis for taxation, by narrowing the definition of "related businesses" for tax purposes, by imposing various expenses on nonprofit providers, and by reducing the relative incentives for charitable contributions (pp. 24-25).

5. In addition to a fiscal crisis, nonprofit organizations also face a broader *economic crisis* (pp. 28-37):

• To survive the budget cuts and the slow growth in private giving during the 1980s, nonprofit organizations turned increasingly to fees and charges for their services. Well over half (52 percent) of the growth that the nonprofit sector experienced during the 1980s was financed from this source, compared to 8 percent from private giving (p. 28).

• Now for-profit providers are increasingly entering these fields and successfully competing against the nonprofit providers. For-profit firms expanded rapidly in the hospital field in the 1980s, and have outpaced nonprofits in home health and other human services. In home health, for example, for-profits accounted for all of the growth in establishments and 74 percent of the growth in employment between 1977 and 1992 (pp. 29-33).

• The resulting competition has put a squeeze on some of the "mission-related" activities that have made nonprofits distinctive (e.g., charity care, research, training) and raised questions about the viability of the nonprofit form.

• Reflecting this, nonprofit hospitals are converting to for-profit status or being absorbed by for-profit chains in record numbers (p. 31). In addition, nonprofit social service agencies are being pulled into increasingly commercial pursuits, and similar pressures are evident in arts, culture, and higher education (pp. 34-36).

6. The nonprofit sector is also increasingly confronting a *crisis of accountability* as serious new questions are being asked about the *effectiveness* of nonprofit activities. This is a product in part

of the general assault that is underway against government social programs. In addition, it reflects a reaction against what some see as the overprofessionalization of human services and the lack of adequate performance measures and accountability mechanisms in the nonprofit sector (pp. 37-41).

7. Finally, and perhaps most seriously, the nonprofit sector is experiencing a serious *crisis of legitimacy.* This is partly a result of a recent spate of highly publicized scandals. But it is also the conse-quence of a growing mismatch between the way the sector actually operates and the quaint nineteenth-century image that dominates public understanding (pp. 41-46).

- Reflecting this, only a third of the population expresses "a great deal" or "quite a lot" of confidence in nonprofit organizations outside of religion and education.

- Serious challenges have recently arisen to the tax-exempt status of these organizations at the local level, to the establishment of nonprofit agencies in particular locales, and to the ability of these organizations to engage in public advocacy (pp. 43-46).

8. While serious challenges confront the American nonprofit sector at the present time, a number of *countervailing trends* are also evident:

- New grass-roots organizations continue to form to cope with homelessness, hunger, AIDS, joblessness, polution, and many other issues (pp. 49-50).

- Despite recent fears of a deterioration in civic activity, there is substantial evidence of continued civic participation (pp. 50-51).

- An extraordinary $10 trillion is projected to be transferred via inheritance from the Depression-era generation to the postwar baby boomers over the next 20 to 40 years, creating potentially substantial opportunities for expanding charitable bequests (p. 51).

• A new mode of *corporate involvement in community affairs* is taking shape that integrates corporate social responsibility more firmly into the strategic operations of companies in ways that make corporate managers available to nonprofit organizations for new types of collaborations (pp. 52-53).

9. Encouraging though they are, however, these countervailing trends will not offset the challenges that exist. Nor is it possible to turn the clock back to a mythical nineteenth-century "golden age" of voluntarism. Rather, to cope with the challenges that confront the nonprofit sector, a sensible strategy of *renewal* is needed (pp. 55-58).

• Central to such a strategy is acceptance of the "partnership model" of nonprofit operations, the view that nonprofit organizations can usefully pursue their special role in partnership with government and the business sector (p. 57).

• More generally, renewal requires a re-examination of the nonprofit sector's basic values and beliefs in light of contemporary realities. Traditional notions of philanthropy and altruism must come to terms with new impulses for empowerment, self-realization, and self-help—for citizen involvement and engagement in societal problem-solving. This may require new vehicles for nonprofit action and new legal approaches— for example, a loosening, rather than a tightening, of existing prohibitions on nonprofit advocacy (p. 58).

• To implement such a renewal process, several steps could usefully be taken:
— Explore a number of concrete actions that could reconnect the nonprofit sector with its citizen base (pp. 59-60);
— Establish a series of state-level Civil Society Commissions with the aid of the existing nonprofit "infrastructure organizations," including those at the state and local level, to review these ideas, to rethink the basic values and operations of the nonprofit sector, and to forge a new consensus about the role this sector plays and the way it should function in the years ahead (p. 60);

— Launch a major media campaign to educate the public about this sector and the way it collaborates with government and business to enrich our public life and address our public problems (pp. 60-61).

10. Fortunately, some of these steps are already being explored. They must now be even more vigorously pursued. While the nonprofit sector may have enough resilience to survive even the challenges outlined in this report without concerted action, the sector is too important to risk relying on a policy of drift. Pro-active initiative is required.

Additional copies of this report, Lester M. Salamon, *Holding the Center: America's Nonprofit Sector at a Crossroads* (New York: The Nathan Cummings Foundation, 1997), are available free of charge from The Nathan Cummings Foundation, 1926 Broadway, Suite 600, New York, NY 10023 / Fax: 212-787-7377.

# Holding the Center

America's Nonprofit Sector at a Crossroads

# Introduction

America has long had a special love affair with its private nonprofit sector. But like all such relationships, this one has been characterized by far more tension and complexity than either party would probably prefer to admit. Complaints about the "nonprofit sector" even intruded into town meeting debates over the ratification of the U.S. Constitution, as citizens faulted Harvard College—America's first nonprofit corporation—for shortcomings that sound hauntingly similar to ones being lodged against nonprofit institutions today—elitism, unresponsiveness, and lack of public accountability.[1] At the very time that Alexis de Tocqueville was celebrating the penchant for association as one of the defining features of American democracy, in fact, state legislatures throughout the young republic were denying charitable institutions the basic right to incorporate and forbidding courts from assuming the enforcement powers needed to make charitable endowments feasible.[2]

Not until the late nineteenth century, in fact, was America's deep-seated ambivalence toward nonprofit corporations replaced with the more reverential attitude that has come down to us today. When this change occurred, however, it was as part of a broader movement to legitimize private corporate activity and protect it from governmental control. As a consequence, the nonprofit sector was quickly enveloped in ideology and the reality of nonprofit operations shrouded by a pervasive myth of voluntarism and a resulting set of popular expectations that few merely human institutions could hope to fulfill.

Now, as the twentieth century draws to a close, it appears that the nonprofit sector is in danger of reaping the whirlwind to which this elevated position has exposed it. Major new challenges have arisen in recent years to the fiscal and moral position of the nonprofit sector. These challenges are taking place, moreover, against a backdrop of intense economic pressures and growing doubts about the legitimacy of the whole concept of nonprofit activity.

Any one of these developments by itself would pose serious questions about the future of this set of institutions. The fact that they are all hitting simultaneously, however, makes the questioning all the more profound. While opinions can legitimately differ over whether the resulting situation constitutes a true "crisis" for America's nonprofit sector, it seems clear that a challenge of potentially historic proportions is at hand.

The purpose of this report is to offer a preliminary overview of the major dimensions of this challenge and to suggest why it should be a matter of general concern. Based on interviews with more than a dozen close observers of the American nonprofit scene, a set of background memos commissioned from experts on particular facets of this sector (health, social services, arts, taxation), and a review of a substantial body of recent data and related material, the report identifies four broad sets of challenges confronting the American nonprofit sector at the present time and explores each one in turn. It then examines a number of potentially counterbalancing developments that could offer some relief. Finally, against this backdrop, it suggests some steps that could usefully be taken to renew the sector and reinvigorate its popular base.

# CHAPTER I

# Background: The Stakes

Before examining the difficult challenges confronting America's nonprofit sector at the present time, it may be useful to review briefly what this set of institutions is and why its future is appropriately a matter of concern. This is particularly important in view of the fact that much of the current assault on this sector is fueled by profound misunderstandings about what the sector does, what types of institutions it contains, and what role it plays in our national life.

## What is the Nonprofit Sector?

Although the basic character of the nonprofit sector is described elsewhere,[3] it may be useful to bear several salient facts in mind:

- That America's nonprofit, or tax-exempt, sector is a significant presence in our national life, embracing approximately 1.4 million *organizations* with operating expenditures of some $500 billion as of 1993.[4] Indeed, the nonprofit sector accounts for:
    — half of all our hospitals;
    — half of all colleges and universities;
    — almost all of our symphony orchestras;
    — 60 percent of our social service agencies;
    — most of our civic organizations.

- That despite many differences, the entities in this sector also share at least five key characteristics. In particular, they are: (i) *organizations*; (ii) that are *not part of the governmental apparatus*; (iii) that *do not distribute profits to their directors*; (iv) that are *self-governing*; and (v) that serve some *public purpose* that has been

judged by the U.S. Congress, and by many state and local legislatures, to entitle them to full or partial exemption from many
forms of taxation.

• That within this sector are two rather different sets of institutions, one of which is essentially *member-serving*, i.e., primarily
devoted to serving the members of the organization; and the
other of which is essentially *public-serving*, i.e., dedicated to
serving the public at large. This broad distinction is reflected in
American tax law, which accords all nonprofit organizations
exemption from federal income tax, but restricts to the public-
serving organizations, and really to the subset of them that does
not engage significantly in "lobbying" activity, the privilege to
receive tax-deductible gifts, i.e., contributions that the donors
can deduct from their income in computing their tax liabilities.
*It is this latter set of "charitable" public-benefit organizations, plus the
closely related public-serving "action" agencies, that therefore forms the
heart of the nonprofit sector, and that will be our principal focus here.*

• That this public-serving portion of the nonprofit sector
itself embraces many different types of entities. These include
churches, foundations, environmental groups, civic organizations, and a wide assortment of service agencies providing
everything from health care to education to housing for the
homeless to information on crucial unmet needs.

• That, excluding churches, this public-serving portion of the
nonprofit sector by itself had expenditures as of 1992 of
approximately $392 billion. This represents approximately 6.5
percent of the U.S. gross national product and exceeds the
gross national products of all but a dozen countries, including
Mexico, Argentina, Australia, India, and the Netherlands.

• That these expenditures are heavily concentrated in the health
component of the sector, which alone accounts for
61 percent of the total; and in education, which accounts for
another 22 percent. The lion's share of the organizations,
however, is in the fields of social services, civic action, and

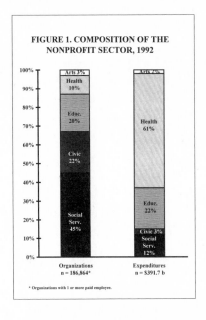

**FIGURE 1. COMPOSITION OF THE NONPROFIT SECTOR, 1992**

Organizations
n = 186,864*

Expenditures
n = $391.7 b

* Organizations with 1 or more paid employee.

mutual aid (see Figure 1). Indeed, there are hundreds of thousands of nonprofit organizations with fewer than one paid staff member that do not even show up in these figures but that form a critical component of community life.

## The Contributions of the Nonprofit Sector

The contributions of the non-profit sector go well beyond what even these impressive economic indicators might suggest, however. In particular, it is possible to identify at least *four distinctive types of contributions* that nonprofit organizations make to American society. While these contributions may not be unique to this sector, they are certainly particularly characteristic of it. They therefore define the stakes that Americans have in this set of institutions.

*Value Guardian*

Perhaps most fundamentally, the nonprofit sector functions as a "value guardian" in American society, as an exemplar and crucial embodiment of a fundamental national value emphasizing *individual initiative in the public good*. Just as private economic enterprises serve as vehicles for promoting individual initiative for the private good, nonprofit organizations provide a mechanism for promoting such initiative in the pursuit of *public* purposes. In the process, they foster pluralism, diversity, and freedom. These values go beyond the more instrumental purposes that nonprofit organizations also serve, such as improving health or providing shelter to the homeless. They are important in and of themselves, as expressions of what has come to be regarded as a central dimension of the American experience— the protection of a sphere of private action through which individuals can take the initiative, express their individuality, and exercise freedom of expression and action.

*Service Provision*

Nonprofits not only embody crucial values, however. They are also active in providing solutions. The nonprofit sector has functioned as a first line of defense, a flexible mechanism through which people concerned about a social or economic problem can begin to respond immediately without having to convince a majority of their fellow citizens that the problem deserves a more general, governmental response. It also provides a vehicle through which publicly financed services themselves can be delivered, thereby avoiding the enlargement of governmental bureaucracies and keeping the provision of services in private institutions at the community level. The nonprofit sector has thus been particularly important to persons in need, to populations lacking the resources to purchase critical goods and services such as health care, food, and shelter, on which their survival depends. The sector's organizations do so by channeling resources from other portions of society or by fostering self-help and mutual support among the needy themselves.

Nonprofits are also available to provide "collective goods" that only a portion of a community considers essential, thus overcoming the inherent limitations of both the market and the state in responding to such needs. Thus nonprofits are often active in the cultural sphere or in recreation, in promoting environmental improvement or providing education. Even where government has been persuaded to act, moreover, nonprofit organizations still often perform a vital service role by making it possible to deliver services in a more flexible fashion, in a smaller setting, with greater local input. In short, nonprofits perform a vital service role by:

- addressing unmet needs;
- fostering innovation;
- providing "collective goods" that only a portion of a community wishes to support; and
- adapting general policies to local circumstances and needs.

*Advocacy and Problem-Identification*

In addition to solving problems themselves, nonprofit organizations also play a vital role as mechanisms for mobilizing broader public attention to societal problems and needs. In this sense, they give crucial support to another basic value, the value of free expression. In a complex society such as ours, the right to free expression has little effective meaning unless it is joined to the right of free association, so that individuals can merge their individual voices and thereby make them effective. Nonprofit organizations are among the principal vehicles for doing this. Indeed, most of the social and political movements that have animated American life over the past half century or more—the women's suffrage movement, the labor movement, the civil rights movement, the environmental movement, the consumer movement, the equal rights movement, and now the conservative movement—have operated through private, nonprofit organizations. By making it possible to surface significant social and political concerns, to give voice to under-represented people and points of view, and to integrate these perspectives into social and political life, these organizations function as a kind of social safety valve that has helped to preserve American democracy and maintain a degree of social peace in the midst of massive, and often dramatic, social dislocations.

*Social Capital*

Finally, nonprofit organizations play a vital role in creating and sustaining what scholars have come to refer to as "social capital," i.e., those bonds of trust and reciprocity that seem to be pivotal for a democratic society and a market economy to function effectively, but that the American ethic of individualism would otherwise make it difficult to sustain.[5] Alexis de Tocqueville understood this point well when he wrote in *Democracy in America* in 1835:

> *Feelings and opinions are recruited, the heart is enlarged, and the human mind is developed, only by the reciprocal influence of men upon one another....[T]hese influences are almost null in democratic countries; they must therefore be artificially created and this can only be accomplished by associations.*[6]

The perpetuation of a vital nonprofit sector is thus essential to the development and sustenance of a sense of community, which is required to uphold contracts and make it possible for both a market system and a democratic polity to operate.

# CHAPTER 2

# The Current Crisis

For a variety of reasons, this set of institutions that is so crucial to the preservation of the American experience now faces an extraordinary series of challenges. Each of these challenges by itself would tax the staying power of this sector. What makes the current situation particularly troubling is that several different challenges are hitting the sector at once. The degrees of freedom available to nonprofit managers are therefore declining dramatically, leading many to give up on the nonprofit form altogether.

To be sure, this is not the first time that the nonprofit sector has confronted significant challenges. Nor do the current challenges affect all components of this sector to the same extent. Nonprofit universities and symphony orchestras may be in a far different position from small soup kitchens and homeless shelters. Side-by-side with the evidence of distress, moreover, are more positive signs as well. Gauging the state of health of the nonprofit sector is therefore a complex task requiring a careful sifting of a wide assortment of evidence.

Based on such a sifting, it seems clear to this author that an unusual series of challenges *does* confront the American nonprofit sector at the present time, that these challenges affect a significant portion of the sector, and that considerable harm could be done to a set of institutions in which Americans have a crucial stake if these challenges are not effectively addressed. More particularly, four such challenges seem especially prevalent. Together they constitute an emerging crisis of the American nonprofit sector.

## The Fiscal Crisis

The most visible of these crises is fiscal in character: *Key portions of the nonprofit sector face a continuing decline in one of their most important sources of support—i.e., government revenue—and seem unlikely to be able to make it up from the source that is widely assumed to be the most likely alternative—i.e., private charitable giving.* This is taking place, moreover, at a time of increased need for the services that nonprofits provide.

*Background: Nonprofit Federalism*

To understand the nature of this challenge, it is necessary to review briefly the recent history of nonprofit finances. Perhaps the most salient feature of this history has been the vast expansion of governmental support to nonprofit organizations, particularly during the 20 years that began with the Great Society era of the mid-1960s. Faced with expanding pressures to alleviate the serious poverty and distress that became increasingly visible in the late 1950s and early 1960s, the federal government responded with a host of new programs that relied extensively on private, nonprofit organizations for their implementation. The result was the emergence of an elaborate and widespread partnership between government and the nonprofit sector in a wide variety of fields.[7]

Though it is not generally recognized, this development was far from unprecedented. Despite a widespread belief in a mythical "golden age" of purely voluntary involvement and wholly private philanthropic support, a rich, and largely productive, collaboration has existed between nonprofit organizations and government from the very beginning of this nation. The first nonprofit corporation on American soil, Harvard College, was established by an act of the General Court of the Massachusetts Bay Colony in the mid-1600s, and the colonial government not only chartered the college but also provided it with £400 in capital and a dedicated tax, the "colledge corne," for operating support.[8] This pattern is mirrored, moreover, in the early histories of many other premier private nonprofit institutions, such as Yale University, Dartmouth College, and the Metropolitan Museum of Art.[9] Until the latter nineteenth century, in fact, nonprofit organizations were thought of as part of the "public sector" because they contributed to the solution of public problems. As the problems of poverty and distress grew in American cities in the late nineteenth century, it was therefore natural for government and private charities to respond in a similar fashion, through a variety of collaborative ties. Many of the private charitable institutions now being touted by conservative theorists as exemplars of "effective compassion"[10] were thus able to carry out their work thanks in large part to government aid:

- Of 28 private charities for poor children in New York in the latter 1870s, for example, only 11 percent were entirely supported by private charity. Fully 60 percent received *over half* of their support from state and local government funds, and another 29 percent received up to half of their support from this same source.[11]

- Throughout the latter nineteenth century, in fact, New York City regularly channeled a portion of its excise taxes on liquor and tobacco to more than 100 charitable organizations, including the (mostly Protestant) New York Association for Improving the Condition of the Poor, the (Roman Catholic) Society of St. Vincent de Paul, and the United Hebrew Charities.

- Nor was this phenomenon limited to New York. A turn-of-the-century survey of social welfare programs found such government-nonprofit partnerships operating in all but four western states.[12] Indeed, the very first *federal* social service program took this same form—i.e., a grant-in-aid to a private, nonprofit home for the elderly, the Little Sisters of the Poor, located in Washington, D.C. And this program was enacted in 1872!

Confronted with pervasive distress that private charity alone could not handle, local officials thus resorted to the tax system to raise funds, but then turned much of the resulting revenue over to nonprofit institutions to care for those in need. The upshot was an extensive pattern of government-nonprofit cooperation.

While cooperation between government and the nonprofit sector is deeply rooted in American history, however, it expanded massively in the 1960s and 1970s when the federal government entered the scene in response to continued poverty and distress, limited growth in private charitable support, and a changed political climate. Rather than pursue wholly governmental initiatives, however, the social programs of the Great Society adhered to the prevailing pattern of government reliance on private, nonprofit groups. The major innovation of the Great Society, therefore, was not to invent a new pattern for carrying out governmental human service responsibilities, but to mobilize the resources of the federal government behind a pattern that was already in widespread use locally.

Given the scale of federal involvement, moreover, the result was dramatic. This is evident in the history of the nation's family service agencies, one of the few components of the nonprofit sector for which we have reliable data over time. As recently as 1967, United Way and sectarian fund drives provided well over half (60 percent) of the income of the typical family service agency, compared to 14 percent from government and 26 percent from fees, charges, and related sources. By 1985, the government share had risen from 14 percent to 36 percent, and the share from private charitable

TABLE I

### Sources of Nonprofit Income, 1977

| | % of Income from | | | |
| | Private Giving | Government | Fees Charges | Total |
|---|---|---|---|---|
| Health | 11% | 35% | 54% | 100% |
| Education, Research | 15 | 18 | 67 | 100 |
| Social Services | 33 | 54 | 13 | 100 |
| Civic, Fraternal | 31 | 50 | 19 | 100 |
| Arts, culture | 41 | 12 | 47 | 100 |
| **Total** | **18%** | **31%** | **51%** | **100%** |

Source: Computed from data in Hodgkinson, Weitzman et. al. *Nonprofit Almanac* (1992)

support had dropped to around 35 percent.[13] Elsewhere, the growth of government support was even more striking. Indeed, as Table 1 shows, by 1977, government support to nonprofit organizations exceeded private charitable support by nearly 2:1. And among social service and civic and fraternal organizations, the government share topped 50 percent.

Nor did this growth of government support come at the expense of private charitable support, as some have suggested. Private giving continued to grow throughout this period at roughly its historical rate.[14] But government support grew more robustly. Far from reducing nonprofit activity, therefore, government funding actually fueled its expansion, enlarging the nonprofit sector and enabling it to extend its reach. In fact, a survey conducted in the early 1980s revealed that three-fifths of all nonprofit human service agencies in existence as of 1982 had been created since 1960, during the period of most rapid governmental expansion.[15] In place of a conflict between government and nonprofit organizations, in other words, what emerged was an elaborate, and extensive, partnership instead.

*The Reagan Cutbacks*

Against this background, the election of Ronald Reagan in 1980 produced a significant reversal. Justifying its moves as an effort to get government out of the nonprofit sector's way, the Reagan administration significantly reduced government spending in many of the fields where nonprofits are active. In the process, however, it also reduced a significant source of nonprofit revenue and hence the ability of nonprofit organizations to meet the expanded need. Although federal spending continued to grow in the health field, elsewhere it declined by approximately 25 percent in the early 1980s and had not returned to its 1980 level in inflation-adjusted terms by fiscal year 1994. Indeed, as of 1994, federal spending was still below 1980 levels in:

— education and social services (down 19 percent);
— international assistance (down 17 percent); and
— community development (down 42 percent).

Although spending in many of these fields began to increase again in the late 1980s and early 1990s, nonprofit organizations outside of the health field nevertheless lost a cumulative total of $38 billion in federal revenue between 1982 and 1994 compared to what they would have had available if 1980 spending levels had been maintained. At the same time, overall federal spending in these fields initially declined by 12-13 percent below 1980 levels and did not return to its 1980 level until 1991. This translated into a substantial increase in the service demands nonprofit organizations were called on to meet. Furthermore, while federal health spending continued to increase, a shift in the Medicare reimbursement system toward pre-fixed payments instead of cost-based reimbursement created powerful pressures for cost reduction in the health sphere as well.

*The "Contract With America" Cuts*

With the election of a Republican majority in Congress in 1994, the pressures on nonprofit revenues from government returned with a vengeance. Committed through their *Contract with America* not only to eliminate the Reagan-era federal deficit but also to accommodate a further massive tax cut, Republican budget planners targeted not only the "discretionary" programs that had been the object of Reagan-era cuts, but key facets of the Federal government's "entitlement" protections as well, including Medicaid, Medicare, and Aid to Families with Dependent Children.[16] Thus, the Congressional budget resolution that passed in the summer of 1995 projected cumulative cuts of $355 billion *below actual FY 1995 levels* in federal spending during FY 1996-2002 in fields of primary interest to nonprofit organizations. Despite presidential resistance, moreover, the Republican majority made considerable headway in putting this plan into action. In particular, the appropriations bills finally enacted for the 1996 fiscal year reduced spending on discretionary programs of interest to nonprofit organizations by 12 percent, or some $8.5 billion, below what was spent in fiscal year 1995. In some fields, moreover, the cutbacks were even more severe. Thus, spending was reduced in this one year:

- by 17 percent for the Social Services Block Grant;
- by 20 percent for post-secondary student assistance;
- by 24 percent for disadvantaged housing;
- by 26 percent for community service;
- by 32 percent for the Legal Services Corporation; and
- by 34 percent for low-income energy assistance.

These cutbacks reduced federal support for nonprofit organizations under these programs by an estimated $1.7 billion, or about 10 percent, in FY 1996 alone. In addition to this, the welfare reform bill adopted in the summer of 1996 eliminated one of the major entitlement programs providing assistance to the poor, thus potentially putting further demand on the services available through nonprofit organizations.[17]

While other political developments during 1996, such as the successful presidential standoff with Congress over the budget and the subsequent voter rejection of the tax-cut program advanced by candidate Dole, have reduced the fiscal pressures nonprofits are likely to face, moreover, they have hardly eliminated these pressures entirely. For one thing, despite the remarkable political recovery of President Clinton, the political forces that produced a politics of budgetary stringency in 1995 and 1996 appear more entrenched now than they were in the 1980s. Thus, while handing President Clinton a stunning electoral victory in 1996, voters returned Republican majorities in both the House and Senate, and even boosted the Republican margin in the latter. Among other things, this may increase the chances that a balanced budget amendment to the federal constitution will be passed and sent to the states for ratification. Such an amendment came close to passage in 1995 but was rejected by a narrow margin in the Senate, largely because of the opposition of Republican Senator Mark Hatfield of Oregon, who has now retired.

Complicating matters further, while state governments proved able to offset at least some of the cutbacks in federal discretionary spending during the 1980s, this time the advocates of retrenchment are firmly ensconced at the state level as well, even in states such as New York and New Jersey that have traditionally supported generally progressive social policies. Indeed, the number of states with Democratic governors stands at only 17 today, compared to 27 in 1981; and the number of states with Democratic majorities in both houses of the legislature has fallen from 29 in 1981 to 20 today. All of these factors increase the likelihood that cuts at the federal level will be sustained in the states.

These developments are especially significant in view of budget projections suggesting a continuation of significant federal deficits if no corrective action is taken, although the deficit for fiscal year 1996 has turned out to be much smaller than originally projected.[18] Since a tacit agreement seems to have been forged between the President and Congress to achieve budgetary balance by the year 2002, further downward pressure on discretionary spending and potentially significant reductions in the growth of entitlement spending still seem likely. This is particularly so in view of the fact that both the President and Congress appear committed to some sort of short-term tax relief, even if it takes the form of the targeted cuts the President put forward in the 1996 campaign.

The scope of the reductions that will be needed are far from certain as of this writing, of course. However, the FY 1997 budget resolution that Congress passed in the summer of 1996 provides the most recent official estimate. According to this resolution, federal spending on programs of interest to nonprofit organizations would be cut a cumulative total of $216 billion over the FY 1997-2002 period below what would have been available had FY 1995 levels remained in place. By the year 2002 under this resolution, the value of federal social service spending would thus decline 25 percent below what it was in FY 1995, the value of community development spending would decline by 51 percent, and the value of international aid spending would decline by 48 percent (See Table 2).

These projected reductions in federal spending mean further increases in the demands on nonprofit agencies. At the same time, however, they also mean further reductions in the *revenues* nonprofit agencies have available to meet those demands. Thus, as shown in Table 3 on page 20, the FY 1997 budget resolution projects an 18 percent reduction below FY 1995 levels in the inflation-adjusted

TABLE 2

## Projected Changes in Federal Spending on Programs
## of Interest to Nonprofit Organizations, FY 1997-2002,

FY 1997 Congressional Budget Resolution

vs. FY 1995 Levels (in billions of FY 1995 dollars)

| Budget Function | Projected FY 2002 Spending vs. Actual FY 1995 | | Cumulative Change FY 1997-2002 vs. FY 1995 |
|---|---|---|---|
| | Amount | % | |
| Education, social services | $-13.1 | -25% | -$66.1 |
| Community Development | -5.4 | -51% | -$20.8 |
| Health | -47.3 | -16% | -$149.3 |
| Income Assistance | +12.3 | +4 | +$52.1 |
| International | -7.4 | -48% | -$32.1 |
| Total | -$60.9 | -11% | -$216.2 |
| Excluding Income Assistance | -$73.2 | -12% | -$268.3 |

Source: Alan J. Abramson and Lester M. Salamon, "FY 1997 Federal Budget: Implications for the Nonprofit Sector," (June 1996).

value of federal support to nonprofit organizations as of FY 2002. Indeed, if Congress follows the guidelines it has established for itself in this budget resolution, nonprofit organizations stand to lose a cumulative total of close to $90 billion in Federal support over the FY 1997-2002 period. This would significantly reduce federal support to nonprofit organizations in such fields as education and training, employment, social services, community development, health, international assistance, and arts and culture.

While it is far from clear whether the proposals outlined in this resolution will be enacted, and while not all nonprofit organizations would be affected even if they were, the likelihood of continued fiscal pressures on a considerable portion of the nonprofit sector thus appears very high.

*Constraints on Private Charitable Growth*

To what extent can we reasonably expect increases in private giving to offset these reductions in federal expenditures on programs of interest to nonprofit organizations, and ultimately in federal support to nonprofit organizations, as advocates of the cuts have hoped? The answer, it seems, is not very much. For one thing, the scale of increases required is overwhelming. As reflected in Figure 2, in order to offset just the direct revenue losses that nonprofits will endure if even the FY 1997 Congressional Budget Resolution, let alone the original *Contract with America* Budget Resolution, is implemented, private giving would have to grow by 12 percent above the rate of inflation in fiscal year 1997, by 16 percent in fiscal year 1998, and by 32 percent as of fiscal year 2002. Yet the recent growth has rarely exceeded the inflation rate by even 3 percent. In short, although the cuts that now seem likely are considerably

TABLE 3

**Projected Changes in Nonprofit Revenues
from Federal Sources, FY 1997-2002**

FY 1997 Congressional
Budget Resolution vs. Actual FY 1995 Spending
(in billions of 1995 dollars)

| | Proposed vs. FY 1995 Actual | | Cumulative Change Proposed FY 1997-2002 vs. FY 1995 |
|---|---|---|---|
| | Amount | % | |
| Education, Training, Social Services | -3.6 | -24% | -$13.1 |
| Community and Regional Development | -0.4 | -51% | -1.4 |
| Health | -19.7 | -17% | -67.6 |
| International Affairs | -0.5 | -45% | -2.0 |
| **Total** | **-$24.1** | **-18%** | **-$89.1** |

Source: Alan J. Abramson and Lester M. Salamon, "FY 1997 Federal Budget: Implications for the Nonprofit Sector," (June 1996).

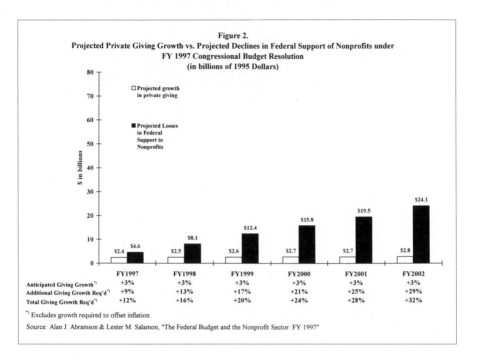

Figure 2.
Projected Private Giving Growth vs. Projected Declines in Federal Support of Nonprofits under
FY 1997 Congressional Budget Resolution
(in billions of 1995 Dollars)

|  | FY1997 | FY1998 | FY1999 | FY2000 | FY2001 | FY2002 |
|---|---|---|---|---|---|---|
| Anticipated Giving Growth[*] | +3% | +3% | +3% | +3% | +3% | +3% |
| Additional Giving Growth Req'd[*] | +9% | +13% | +17% | +21% | +25% | +29% |
| Total Giving Growth Req'd[*] | +12% | +16% | +20% | +24% | +28% | +32% |

[*] Excludes growth required to offset inflation.

Source: Alan J. Abramson & Lester M. Salamon, "The Federal Budget and the Nonprofit Sector: FY 1997"

smaller than the ones in the original *Contract* proposal, giving
would have to grow by anywhere from three times its recent highs
in the early years to 10 times in the latter years in order to fill in
just for the direct revenue losses that nonprofits can expect to
experience. To fill in for the much larger overall reductions in federal spending in these fields, the growth rates will have to increase
by anywhere from five to twenty times.

The history of private giving growth in the 1980s, the last time
giving was called on to offset significant budget cuts, is hardly
encouraging, however. In fact:

• Individual giving as a share of personal income actually
  declined during the 1980s, from an average of 1.81 percent per
  year over the period 1973-82 to 1.76 percent over the period
  1983-1992.[19]

• One reason for this may have been the increase in the standard
  deduction on the federal income tax forms and the resulting
  decline in the share of taxpayers who itemize their deductions,
  including their charitable deductions. Already by 1982, only 35
  percent of all taxpayers itemized their deductions, and only 32

percent claimed charitable deductions. By 1992, the proportion of itemizers was down to 29 percent and the proportion claiming charitable deductions down to 26 percent.[20] Since research has shown that itemizers tend to give more to charity than do non-itemizers, this reduction in the share of taxpayers itemizing their deductions has a negative impact on charitable giving.

• At the same time, the liberalization of tax rates during the 1980s, particularly at the upper income levels, seems to have reduced the incentives to give among upper income taxpayers, who received the greatest benefits from the tax changes. Thus, while the average charitable deduction per return increased by 30 percent in real terms between 1983 and 1992 for all taxpayers, it *declined* by 55 percent for taxpayers with adjusted gross income of $1 million or more, and by 65 percent for taxpayers with adjusted gross income of $500,000 to $1 million.[21] This result runs counter to the hopes of those who claimed that the 1986 tax act, by reducing marginal tax rates for upper income taxpayers and thus leaving more money in their hands, would encourage these taxpayers to contribute more to charity. The actual outcome seems more consistent with econometric models suggesting that when the out-of-pocket "cost" of giving increases, as it does when tax rates fall, the incentive to give declines and giving falls off.

• Changes in tax law also seem to have affected *bequest* giving. The real value of estates grew by some 74 percent between 1977 and 1992. However, the share of all estate returns that made provisions for charitable bequests declined during this period from 22.1 percent to 18.6 percent; and compared to the 74 percent rise in the value of the estates, the value of the charitable bequests from these estates grew by only 19 percent. In other words, well over 80 percent of all estates make no provision for charitable bequests; this share seems to be falling; and so is the share of all estate wealth that finds its way into charitable bequests.[21] This is sobering news indeed for those who have looked to the inter-generational transfer of wealth that now seems to be under way as a source of immense new income for charitable institutions.

• Some growth did occur in both corporate and foundation giving, but these sources are not sufficiently large to offset the individual giving trends, let alone the much larger declines in governmental support. What is more, in the case of corporations, increased giving in the early 1980s was not sustained in the latter 1980s, and actually reversed course and declined in real terms in the early 1990s.

Reflecting these various developments, private giving, far from filling in for government cutbacks, actually lost ground as a source of nonprofit revenue during the decade that began with the Reagan budget cuts. In particular, as reflected in Table 4, giving fell from 15 percent of total nonprofit revenue in 1982 to 11 percent in 1992. In only two fields (civic and culture), in fact, did giving gain ground during this period, but these are relatively small components of the sector.

TABLE 4
## Private Giving as a Share of Nonprofit Revenue
### 1982–92

| Subsector | Private Giving as % of Total Nonprofit Revenues | |
| --- | --- | --- |
| | 1982 | 1992 |
| Health | 11% | 5 |
| Education | 15 | 15 |
| Social Services | 26 | 21 |
| Civic | 31 | 32 |
| Arts, Culture | 40 | 47 |
| **Total** | **15 %** | **11%** |

Private giving includes giving from individuals, foundations, corporations, and bequests.
Source: Computed from data in *Nonprofit Almanac,* 1996

Complicating things further is the fact that the *composition*, as opposed to the scale, of giving does not seem to match the profile of government spending sufficiently to suggest that one could be a substitute for the other *even if the amounts were equivalent*. Generally speaking, giving is greatest where wealth is greatest, rather than where the need is greatest. What is more, much of private giving flows not to those in greatest need but to functions with a significant "amenity" value to the givers (e.g., education, culture). The suburbanization of the American population has, moreover, accentuated this tendency, requiring nonprofits to reproduce in the suburbs the infrastructure they left behind in cities. This is absorbing great amounts of money but with little real growth in service provision, especially for those in greatest need. As one recent study of the flows of charitable support has noted: "In truth, very little of our tax deductible contributions is targeted to the 'truly needy,' especially from outside our own communities. Voluntary organizations have neither the resources to make a dent in our poverty problem nor the infrastructure to act on a national basis."[23]

*Recent Tax Overhaul Proposals*
Despite the recent rhetoric in Congress about the need to devolve power to the local level, moreover, recent proposals for major tax reform would likely impose additional burdens on nonprofit organizations and further reduce the financial incentives for giving. Essentially, these proposals would shift the basis of federal taxation from income to consumption. Not only would this expose nonprofit organizations to taxation on at least some of their activities (since nonprofits "consume" even though they do not "earn" income), but also it could seriously disrupt, and most likely considerably weaken, the current incentives for charitable contributions. For example:

• A proposal by Congressman Armey to replace the federal income tax with a "flat tax" would eliminate the charitable deduction for both individuals and businesses. Coupled with lower marginal tax rates, this change would reduce considerably the current tax incentives for charitable giving. Although advocates claim that the growth in income left in taxpayers' pockets will more than compensate for this result, econometric simulations suggest contributions would likely decline by 10 percent if this proposal were enacted.[24]

- The proposal originally advanced by Senators Nunn and Domenici to replace the federal income tax with a so-called "Value Added Tax" would eliminate the deductibility of charitable contributions for businesses. In addition, by making savings tax deductible, this proposal would make charitable giving relatively less attractive financially, which could be expected to reduce the propensity to give.[25]

- A proposed National Retail Sales Tax would also eliminate the charitable deduction for income, estate, and gift taxes. In addition, it would treat any property or personal services received as a result of contributions or dues to not-for-profit organizations as purchases that would be taxed at their fair market value.[26]

In addition to their likely negative impact on charitable contributions, and hence on the *revenues* of nonprofit organizations, these proposals would also expose nonprofit organizations to direct taxes on some of their activities, thus increasing their *costs*. For example:

- The Armey Flat Tax would impose a 17 percent tax on the fringe benefits provided to nonprofit employees;

- The National Retail Sales Tax would expose nonprofit organizations to a tax on their sales and purchases, including, for example, purchases of medical supplies for disaster relief. In addition, it would require nonprofits to charge the national sales tax on any of their services that are "commercially available," i.e., available from for-profit as well as nonprofit providers.

At this writing, it seems unlikely that any of these overhaul proposals will be enacted in the foreseeable future. At the same time, at least some of the concepts embodied in these proposals may see the light of day. For example, small business leaders seem

likely to push for establishment of a "commerciality test" in deciding which nonprofit activities are subject to taxation. Under such a
provision, any nonprofit activity for which there is a commercially
available alternative would be subject to tax, regardless of whether
it is a "related" or "unrelated" activity. This would be far more
restrictive than current law, which obliges nonprofits to pay taxes
on income from businesses that are "unrelated" to their charitable
mission, but exempts them from tax on business activities that are
"related" to their charitable purposes (e.g., sales of reprints by
museum shops).

*Other Tax Measures*

Beyond these proposals for federal tax restructuring, moreover,
nonprofit organizations are also confronting mounting opposition
to the definition of what constitutes a "charity" for tax purposes,
restricting it, for example, to organizations that primarily or exclu-
sively serve the poor. Hearings seem likely on this question at the
federal level, and this issue has been joined at the state and local
levels as well, as will be detailed more fully below.

While most of the major tax proposals under serious consider-
ation would likely reduce nonprofit income, or increase nonprofit
costs, at least one set of proposals would operate in the opposite
direction. These are the proposals either to replace the current
charitable deduction system, or to augment it, with a system of *tax
credits*. Unlike tax deductions, which deliver their benefits by reducing the taxable income on which taxpayers compute their tax
obligations, tax credits deliver their benefits by directly reducing the
taxes a taxpayer owes by the full amount, or a given fraction of the
amount, of the charitable gift. Under a tax credit, therefore, the tax
benefit resulting from a given gift does not vary with the tax
bracket of the taxpayer, as it does under the current tax deduction
system. For example, presidential candidate Bob Dole proposed a
100 percent credit up to $500 ($1,000 for joint filers) for donations
to organizations directing at least 75 percent of their expenditures
towards the poor. Taxpayers making such contributions would thus
have their taxes reduced dollar-for-dollar until the stated maximum

was reached. While such proposals entail a more powerful incentive for charitable contributions than that embodied in existing law, they also have a number of disadvantages:

- They are typically linked to proposed cuts in government spending, which translate into reduced revenues for nonprofit organizations.

- If unaccompanied by restrictions on the eligible recipients, tax credits could produce a significant shift in the availability of support, away from charities serving the poor and toward charities serving the better-off. This is so because the government support that would be cut flows more fully to agencies serving the disadvantaged than does private charitable support, which tends to flow more extensively to elite institutions with a significant amenity component. To the extent that tax credits are justified as a way to substitute for budget cuts, therefore, restrictions have to be imposed on the types of charities eligible for such credits.

- If restrictions are introduced on the eligible recipients of tax credits to avoid these problems of resource diversion, as is the case with many of the pending proposals, then other problems arise. For one thing, significant administrative and reporting burdens are involved. In addition, divisions could be created within the charitable sector as competition emerges over which types of organizations are truly "charitable" and therefore appropriately eligible for such credits. Beyond this, restricting tax benefits to certain types of "charitable" agencies in the case of tax credits could establish a precedent for restricting the tax exemption of nonprofit organizations more broadly.

Whether these various issues can be worked out in the near term and a tax credit program put in place is far from certain at this writing. More likely is a continued fiscal squeeze, particularly on agencies serving those in greatest need.

## The Economic Crisis

In addition to the fiscal crisis facing nonprofit organizations as a consequence of reduced government support and tepid growth in private giving is a broader economic crisis in which these organizations also find themselves. In fact, these two crises are interrelated. Fiscal pressures resulting from decreased or uncertain government support have induced nonprofit organizations to seek alternative sources of financial support. Finding inadequate support from private charity, they have turned increasingly to fees and service charges, often with quite good effect. Reflecting this shift, far from declining during the decade of the 1980s, the nonprofit sector appears to have performed unusually well. In particular, overall nonprofit revenue rose by 42 percent between 1982 and 1992 after adjusting for inflation, well above the 32 percent growth achieved by the U.S. economy as a whole. What is more, as Figure 3 shows, this growth was not restricted solely to the hospital and health sector, which has traditionally performed better than the economy generally. Indeed, growth was even higher for social service and civic and fraternal organizations. Only education and arts organizations lagged behind the national average.

Several factors seem to lie behind this substantial record of growth. In the first place, as noted above, the budget cuts of the early 1980s did not touch the entitlement programs such as Medicare and Medicaid, which continued to pump resources into the nonprofit sector. Indeed, many social service providers found ways to redefine their services as health-related and to tap into this growing flow of funds. In addition, state and local governments boosted their own levels of support in a number of fields. Finally, some of the cuts of the early 1980s were reversed as the decade wore on.

Even more important than the continued, albeit selective, growth of government support, however, was the substantial growth in fee and service-charge revenue that occurred. As Figure 4 shows, this source alone accounted for 52 percent of the growth of the nonprofit sector during the 1982-92 period. By contrast, private giving accounted for only 8 percent, well below the share with which it started. In short, faced with the possibility of significant

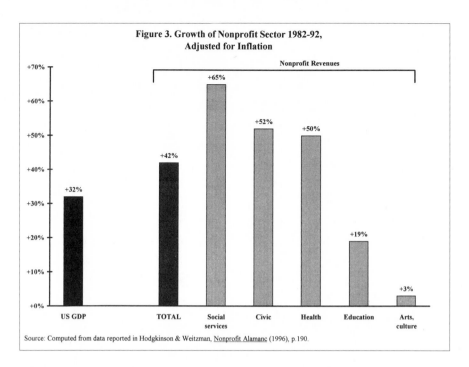

Figure 3. Growth of Nonprofit Sector 1982-92, Adjusted for Inflation

Source: Computed from data reported in Hodgkinson & Weitzman, Nonprofit Alamanc (1996), p.190.

government cutbacks, the nonprofit sector moved much more massively into the commercial market.

While this "marketization" has enabled nonprofit organizations to survive the Reagan-era budget cuts and prosper, it nevertheless has also exposed them to significant new challenges. In a sense, the nonprofit sector may be the victim of its own success. Having created, or newly entered, markets that could yield substantial commercial returns, it is now encountering massive competition from for-profit providers attracted to these same markets. In addition, service purchasers in many of these markets are squeezing profit margins severely, undermining the ability of the nonprofit

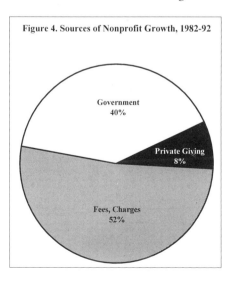

Figure 4. Sources of Nonprofit Growth, 1982-92

providers to subsidize the "mission-related" activities such as charity
care or research that pushed them into these markets in the first
place. This, in turn, has narrowed the differences between the nonprofit and for-profit providers, obscuring the distinctive image of
the nonprofit providers and raising fundamental questions about
the justification for the tax advantages that nonprofit organizations
enjoy. What is more, it has begun to induce nonprofits to convert to
for-profit status in order to attract the capital required to survive. In
this way, through a series of incremental steps, the basic viability of
the nonprofit form appears to be under challenge in a number of
fields. While it may be premature to conclude, paraphrasing T.S.
Eliot, that this is the way the nonprofit sector will end, "not with a
bang but a whimper," the fact remains that numerous nonprofit
organizations are facing serious challenges of precisely this sort.

*Health Care Shifts*
These developments are perhaps most clearly evident in the health
field. Already by 1977, well over half (54 percent) of all nonprofit
health-organization income came from commercial fees and
charges, much of it from third-party insurance payments. Along
with the growth of the federal Medicare and Medicaid programs,
which pumped immense resources into the health care sector, this
commercial activity attracted for-profit providers into the field.
Between 1980 and 1989, in fact, while the overall number of hospitals was declining as a result of competitive pressures in the field,
the number of for-profit hospitals increased by 28 percent, and the
number of beds they control grew by 41 percent. This reflected the
ability of for-profit providers to respond quickly to the demand for
short-term specialty care, while the nonprofit providers remained
tied to the large *general* hospitals where they have historically been
dominant. Of the 239 short-term specialty hospitals added in the
1980s, in fact, over three-quarters were for-profit companies.[27]

While this trend toward for-profit expansion in the hospital
field slowed in the latter 1980s and early 1990s, it has recently
resumed with a vengeance. This time, however, the vehicle is not
the establishment of new for-profit institutions but the take-over of

nonprofit institutions or their conversion into for-profit status. Thus, thirty-one nonprofit hospitals shifted from nonprofit to for-profit status in 1994, usually through acquisitions by for-profit chains; and this number increased to 59 in 1995, with another 200 reported in active discussion.[28] What is more, nonprofit Blue Cross and Blue Shield insurance organizations are under-going similar transformations in major markets from California to New York.[29]

What lies behind these changes is a series of profound shifts in the basic structure of the health care market, which have greatly intensified competitive pressures and put nonprofit providers at a distinct disadvantage. Where formerly providers were compensated for health care services on the basis of their costs or charges, now they are having to negotiate rates with large health maintenance organizations, preferred provider organizations, or other similar mechanisms, which often control large numbers of potential patients and steer them to the lowest-cost providers. Recent estimates put the share of workers in large firms who are in such "managed care" plans at 70 percent, a fundamental turnaround from even five years ago, when such plans embraced only a fraction of the insured population.[30] In addition, the 1983 shift in the federal Medicare program from cost-based reimbursement to a prospective payment system in which rates for certain procedures are set in advance and hospitals are forced to lower their costs to meet these pre-set payments has put further pressures on hospitals' bottom lines. Since nonprofit hospitals subsidized a significant portion of their charity care, research, and teaching from the surplus revenues they received under cost-based reimbursement, these shifts have fundamentally altered their ability to sustain these special mission-related services. Beyond this, the competition for patients coupled with the pressures on the bottom line have necessitated complex consortia arrangements and heavy capital investments in information systems and marketing activities. Because of their inability to offer investors a return on their equity, nonprofit hospitals find it increasingly difficult to compete. This has led some observers to conclude, as one recent article in the *New England Journal of Medicine* put it, that "nonprofit health plans are a byproduct of the past."[31]

While such a conclusion would seem premature, the pressures on nonprofit health providers are severe.

*Human Services*

While the economic pressures on nonprofit health providers are especially salient, similar pressures are also confronting other types of nonprofit organizations, including those providing social services. As noted above, nonprofit social service agencies experienced especially robust growth during the 1980s. One reason for this was the ability of these agencies to tap into the government's health care reimbursement and other entitlement programs to offer home health, day care, and related services. At least as important, however, was the growth of fee income. In fact, fee income accounted for 35 percent of the income growth that social service agencies achieved during the 1980s, compared to only 17 percent from private giving (see Figure 5).

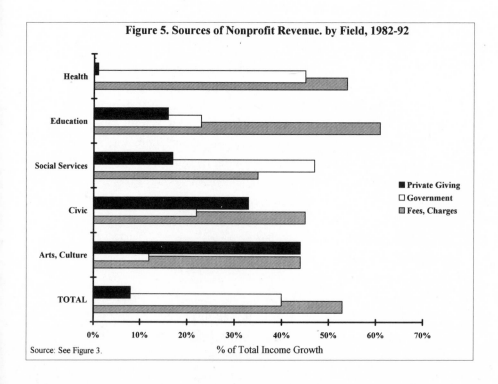

**Figure 5. Sources of Nonprofit Revenue. by Field, 1982-92**

Source: See Figure 3.

% of Total Income Growth

TABLE 5

## For-Profit Expansion in Social Services
## and Home Health Services

1977–92

| Subsector | For Profit Share of | | | |
| --- | --- | --- | --- | --- |
| | Establishments | | Employees | |
| | 1977 | Growth 1977–92 | 1992 | Growth 1977–92 |
| Day Care | 57% | 80% | 46% | 70% |
| Other Social Services | 23% | 30% | 14% | 17% |
| Subtotal, Social Services | 36% | 47% | 21% | 31% |
| Home Health | 44% | 169% | 29% | 74% |

Source: Computed from data in *U.S. Census of Service Industries, 1992*

As with the health care field, however, nonprofit providers have
not been free to pursue these sources of support on their own.
To the contrary, intense competition has emerged from for-profit
providers. What is more, the for-profit providers seem to be gaining
the edge in a number of crucial areas. Thus, as Table 5 shows, for-
profit firms accounted for 80 percent of the growth in *day care*
establishments and 70 percent of the growth in day care employees
between 1977 and 1992, even though they started the period with
only 57 percent of the centers and 46 percent of the employees. In
the *home health* field, one of the most explosive in recent years, for-
profits essentially displaced nonprofit providers during this period,
accounting for all of the growth in establishments and 74 percent
of the growth in employment, although they started the period
with well under 50 percent of both. In *other social services* too, where
nonprofits retain the edge, for-profits have gained ground during
the past decade, accounting for larger shares of the growth than
their presence at the beginning of the period would suggest. It is
therefore no real surprise that the ink was hardly dry on the recent
welfare reform bill before stories began to circulate of huge state

contracts with for-profit companies, including giants like Lockheed Martin and Andersen Consulting, to manage the complex process involved in moving millions of welfare recipients into jobs.[32] In this field, as in many others, the assumption of nonprofit dominance is therefore clearly a thing of the past.

Even where nonprofits have remained competitive, the competition has exacted a price and poses important dilemmas. The case of Family Service America is instructive in this regard. Beginning in 1979, FSA entered into an agreement with the Xerox Corporation to provide substance abuse services to Xerox employees and their families through FSA's network of affiliated agencies. This agreement was soon broadened into a comprehensive employee assistance program covering a wide assortment of emotional concerns on a "managed care" basis, and extended to embrace numerous other corporations, among them General Motors and North American Philips. To cope with the resulting business, which had grown by 1995 to some 75 corporations and annual revenues of $6 million, FSA went through a corporate restructuring in 1992, creating a nonprofit holding company and a for-profit subsidiary known as Family Enterprises, Inc.

Now, however, FSA faces a critical dilemma. While its Family Enterprises operation has proved highly successful, it faces stiff competition from for-profit companies operating in the same field. To remain competitive, it would have to raise significant additional capital. But this would expand the risk exposure of the nonprofit agency. What is more, the preoccupation with servicing the employee assistance contract inevitably detracts from the attention that management staff at FSA and its member agencies can devote to their role as providers of human services to the disadvantaged. Finally, the more effectively they compete with the for-profit firms in their field, the more FSA and its member agencies risk charges of unfair competition from these same firms because of the special tax advantages they enjoy. For nonprofits, it seems, competition is inevitably a two-edged sword, and organizations can as easily fail by succeeding as they can fail by not choosing to play.

*Arts and Education*

Nonprofit arts and education institutions have also found themselves
drawn into difficult competitive dilemmas. For arts institutions, the
significant slowing of federal support along with increased difficulties
in attracting corporate and foundation support have necessitated a
wide variety of innovative "marketing" efforts, including substantial
increases in ticket prices, development of varied outreach programs
at shopping malls or outdoor venues, and the marketing of various
related products, such as books, reproductions of paintings, and
compact discs. In addition, the competition from the commercial
entertainment industry has led many nonprofit groups to emphasize popular, and therefore more remunerative, activities over those
with potentially greater artistic value. Taken together, these activities
are increasingly exposing arts organizations as well to growing
challenges about the legitimacy of their tax exemptions.

The case of higher education is more complex, but also reveal-
ing. As reflected in Figure 2, the growth of nonprofit education has
lagged behind that of other segments of the nonprofit sector. One
reason for this may be the growing resistance to further increases in
college tuition payments, which constitute a particularly important
share of nonprofit higher-education organization revenues. At the
same time, the growth of government support for the research
enterprise at institutions of higher education has slowed considerably in recent years as a consequence of the overall fiscal stringency
and the elimination of the Cold War rationale that helped stimulate
federal research spending in the past.

To offset these fiscal pressures, nonprofit institutions of higher
education, like their counterparts elsewhere in the nonprofit sector,
are increasingly moving into essentially commercial markets.
Medical schools have already paved the way for this in the form of
clinical practice, which provides a significant share of medical
school income nationwide.[33] With the passage of the Dole-Bayh
Bill of 1981, which authorized universities to hold the patent and
licensing rights to discoveries produced with federal funding, new
commercial opportunities have now opened to universities, and
schools are seizing them with considerable energy. At Columbia

University, for example, annual revenues from patents and licenses rose from roughly $4 million to $24 million between the late 1980s and the early 1990s.[34] As part of this general thrust, universities are actively exploring partnerships with private business under which the businesses will invest in university-based research and then share the proceeds of any discoveries that result.

Whether this new commercial involvement by higher education institutions will prove to be blessing or a curse is still far from clear. For one thing, corporate support is likely to be no more reliable than governmental support, and probably less so. Second, heavy reliance on this source of support could seriously distort research priorities and undercut the more basic research that has proved to be the foundation for the success of American higher education. Finally, higher education institutions may find themselves challenged by competing research organizations that can demonstrate more cost-effective ways to carry out the research that corporations need. Indeed, many university professors, newly acquainted with business entrepreneurs, may find it more advantageous to handle their research grants through separate for-profit labs than through the university system, thus denying universities the benefits they seek through these arrangements. If this were to occur on a significant scale, it could fundamentally challenge the whole concept of the modern research university and return the university to its pre-nineteenth-century form as essentially a teaching institution.

*Summary*

In short, the fiscal pressures nonprofits face have induced them to enter fields of activity in which they encounter increasing competition from for-profit providers. In the process, many of the most crucial features of this sector have been put at risk, including the sector's gap-filling role, its willingness to address unmet needs, its innovativeness, its altruism, and its trustworthiness. Indeed, many of these activities have placed nonprofit organizations on a slippery slope that has led them to begin abandoning the nonprofit form altogether. While this may not have negative consequences in the short run, the long-term consequences could be severe, eliminating a crucial element of diversity and weakening a vital mechanism for promoting the values of community.

## The Crisis of Effectiveness

In addition to the fiscal and economic crises facing the nonprofit sector at the present time, a significant *crisis of effectiveness* has surfaced in recent years. Because they do not meet a "market test," nonprofits are always vulnerable to charges that they are inefficient in their use of resources and ineffective in their approaches to problems. The scope and severity of these charges have grown massively in recent years, however. In fact, the competence of the non-profit sector has been challenged on at least three different grounds.

*Programmatic Opposition*

In the first place, nonprofit organizations, particularly in the human service field, have been implicated in the general assault on public social programs that has animated national political debate for more than a decade now. Despite considerable contrary evidence,[35] the persistence of poverty, the alarming growth of urban crime, the epidemic of teen-age pregnancy, and the continuation of welfare dependency have been taken as evidence that these programs not only do not work, but actually make the problems worse. The resulting open season on government social programs has caught major components of the nonprofit sector in the cross-fire, particularly since the sector has been involved in administering many of the programs that are being attacked. Worse than that, the very motives of the nonprofit agencies have been called into question. Involvement in government programs "changes charities' incentives," charges one recent critique, "giving them reasons to keep caseloads up instead of getting them down by successfully turning around peoples' lives."[36] That the assault on these programs has failed to differentiate clearly between the successful and the unsuccessful, that the levels of resources committed to the programs have actually been far less than assumed, and that many of the difficulties these programs have encountered have resulted less from the incapacities of the agencies charged with administering them than with the complex administrative arrangements through which they were forced to operate—all of these factors have not diminished in the least the intensity of the criticisms. In the process, much of the nonprofit human service delivery system has been discredited as a viable instrument for coping with poverty and distress.[37]

### The Professionalization Critique

Beyond the political assault on Great Society social programs lies a more profound line of criticism that takes nonprofit organizations to task for becoming a principal locus for the "overprofessionalization" of societal problem-solving. This line of argument has a long lineage in American social science. In his brilliant history of the social work profession, historian Roy Lubove noted the unfortunate consequences that flowed from the efforts to convert social work into a "profession" in early twentieth-century America. "The motto of the Boston Associated Charities had been 'Not Alms But a Friend,' " Lubove writes. "In the early twentieth century a different concept evolved: neither alms nor a friend, but a professional service."[38] The emergence of a therapeutically oriented casework pattern in social work led social workers away from social diagnosis, community organizing, and social reform—tasks that social workers were uniquely in a position to perform—leaving "a vacuum which remains unfilled."[39] The upshot, widely recognized in the 1960s and 1970s, was a growing alienation of the social work profession and the human service organizations employing them from the impoverished people they were supposed to serve.[40]

A similar process of alienation has been identified in the case of nonprofit hospitals as they were transformed from small community institutions into large, professionalized bureaucracies early in this century. According to one recent analysis of this development:

> As facilities became increasingly large and bureaucratized, and as doctors assumed more responsibilities in the hospital, care became focused less on patients' overall social and moral well-being and more on their physical needs alone....

> *Our modern hospital greatly improved the quality of medical care, but in the process the hospital has lost part of its role as a community institution responsive to social needs that are locally identified.*[41]

This critique of professionalism has gained increased force in recent years, however, as a product of political developments on both the political Left and the political Right. On the Left, the critique of professionalism has figured prominently in the new search for "community." According to this line of thinking, the professionalization of social concerns, by redefining basic human needs as "problems" that only professionals can resolve, has alienated people from the helping relationships they could establish with their neighbors and kin. "Through the propagation of belief in authoritative expertise," Northwestern University Professor John McKnight thus notes, "professionals cut through the social fabric of community and sow clienthood where citizenship once grew."[42] Not only does this undermine community, but it also typically fails to meet the need. Far from fostering social capital and building a sense of community, in other words, nonprofit organizations, by embracing professionalism, have become an enemy of community instead.

Critics on the Right have been equally contemptuous of the professionalized human service apparatus, charging it with inflating the cost of dealing with social problems by "crowding out" lower-cost alternative approaches involving informal networks of families and friends.[43] Similar arguments have been lodged, moreover, against nonprofit educational institutions and cultural institutions. In both cases, the institutions are faulted for being run by and for the professionals who inhabit them rather than for the society that supports them or those, such as students, who need their help.[44]

### The Accountability Movement

Complicating matters further is the fact that nonprofit organizations generally lack meaningful bases for demonstrating the value of what they do. Indeed, nonprofit organizations have often resisted demands for greater accountability on grounds that responding to such demands might interfere with the independence that gives the sector its special character. Instead, nonprofits have tended to point to their not-for-profit status as *ipso facto* evidence of their trustworthiness and effectiveness. Indeed, the trustworthiness supposedly bequeathed by this "nondistribution constraint" has long been one of the principal rationales claimed for the nonprofit form. According to this line of argument, nonprofit organizations are needed precisely to overcome the inherent limitations of the market in situations where information is lacking to allow consumers to make informed choices in the marketplace, and where a higher element of trust is therefore required.[45]

Increasingly, however, these implicit claims by nonprofit providers have been subjected to serious challenge as a result not only of several recent scandals, but also of growing questions about the basic efficiency and effectiveness of nonprofit agencies. "Unlike publicly traded companies," management expert Regina Herzlinger has thus noted, "the performance of nonprofits and governments is shrouded behind a veil of secrecy that is lifted only when blatant disasters occur."[46] This is problematic, she argues, because nonprofit organizations generally lack the three basic accountability mechanisms of business: the self-interest of owners, competition, and the ultimate bottom-line measure of profitability. Although boards of directors are supposed to exercise accountability, in practice this has proved to be a far less effective control device than might be desired. As organizations grow more complex and professional staff members assume greater responsibility, the ability of volunteer boards to exercise effective control declines even with the best of intentions. Nor do the existing reporting requirements on nonprofit organizations offer much help. The Form 990 that no profits must file annually with the Internal Revenue Service contains precious little performance information, and even the basic financial data that organizations file have been found to contain massive error rates. Since the Internal Revenue Service generates no revenue from careful scrutiny of these filings, it naturally devotes little energy to auditing them. Nor do federated fundraising organizations such as United Way systematically review and publicize the performance of their member organizations. Even if they did, the overall impact would be slight since the number of member organizations in any community is quite small.

These concerns have prompted a serious re-evaluation of accountability mechanisms within the nonprofit sector.[47] One line of response has been to strengthen the formal mechanisms for penalizing nonprofit agencies that violate prohibitions against "private inurement," i.e., the use of the nonprofit form for private gain. Thus, in an effort to facilitate greater enforcement of these prohibitions, the Taxpayers' Bill of Rights enacted in the summer of 1996 gives the IRS "intermediate sanctions" in the form of penalty taxes to impose on organizations that violate the "private inurement" rules. However, private inurement is only the most egregious of the accountability problems the nonprofit sector faces, and attention to the other aspects of organizational performance remains a pressing concern.

## Crisis of Legitimacy

Behind the fiscal, economic, and competence issues facing the nonprofit sector at the present time, finally, is a much more fundamental moral or political challenge, a veritable crisis of legitimacy that has raised basic questions about the whole concept of the nonprofit sector and about the sector's entitlement to the special tax and other advantages it enjoys.

In a sense, the nonprofit sector's success at adjusting to the realities of postwar American society may ironically be costing it the support of significant elements of the American public, who remain wedded to a nineteenth-century image of charity and altruism, of small voluntary groups ministering to the needy and downtrodden. The nonprofit sector is thus being hoisted on its own mythology. Having failed to make clear to the American public what its role should be in a mature mixed economy, the sector has been thrown on the defensive by revelations that it is not operating the way its own mythology would suggest. A massive gap has thus opened between the modern reality of a sector intimately involved with government and moving into commercial activities in the wake of governmental cutbacks, and the popular image of a set of

community-based institutions mobilizing purely voluntary energies
to assist those in need. Against this backdrop, disclosures of the sort
involved in the United Way and New Era Philanthropy scandals, and
revelations about the salaries of some nonprofit executives, have fall-
en on unusually fertile ground. The upshot has been a series of fundamental challenges to the sector's credibility and privileged position. These challenges are evident in at least four different forums.

*Public Attitudes*

In the first place, there is evidence of a deterioration in public
confidence in charitable institutions. Recent Gallup surveys of
giving and volunteering reveal that as of 1994 only about one-third
of the American population expressed "a great deal" or "quite a
lot" of confidence in nonprofit organizations outside of religion
and education (see Table 6). This is well above the 19 percent who
expressed this level of confidence in the Federal Government
and the 21 percent who had "a great deal" or "quite a lot" of
confidence in state governments. But it still lagged far behind the
47 percent confidence levels the Federal Government enjoyed in
1975, and the 53 percent and 49 percent levels that small businesses
and the military enjoyed as of 1994.[48]

This apparent weakening of the attachment Americans feel
towards private charitable institutions has not been entirely
spontaneous. It has been encouraged by a strident conservative
assault against key components of the nonprofit sector. Conservative
critics have come to recognize the significant role that nonprofit
organizations have played in surfacing public problems and mobilizing public support for their resolution. Rather than applauding this
crucial advocacy function of nonprofit organizations as a sign of the
vibrancy of American democracy, however, they deplore it as a
potent mechanism for fueling the continued growth of the modern
welfare state. Entire organizations have thus been formed to
challenge the presumed emergence of a "new kind of nonprofit
organization, dedicated not to voluntary action, but to an expanded
government role in our lives."[49] Attacks on nonprofit organizations
have thus become a staple of conservative talk radio and fodder for

TABLE 6

**Public Attitudes Toward Nonprofit Organizations**

1994

| Institution | % Expressing "A Great Deal" or "Quite a Lot" of Confidence |
|---|---|
| Small business | 53% |
| The military | 49 |
| Private higher education | 48 |
| Health organizations | 36 |
| Human service organizations | 33 |
| State government | 21 |
| Federal government | 19 |

Source: Independent Sector, *Giving and Volunteering*, 1994, p. 54.

conservative columnists. Of special focus, moreover, has been the growth of government-nonprofit cooperation, which, in the eyes of conservative critics, has transformed nonprofit organizations into just another group of supplicants "feasting at the public trough" and therefore unable to represent the public interest with objectivity.[50] Given this kind of assault, it is perhaps no wonder that significant portions of the public might begin to question what the nonprofit sector truly represents.

*Tax Exemption Challenge*
Growing public skepticism about the nonprofit sector has in turn played into the hands of hard-pressed state and local governments eager to find new sources of revenue for their own operations. Squeezed by the same budget cuts and growing service needs that are affecting nonprofit organizations, state and local governments have increasingly begun looking at tax-exempt charitable institutions as a potential source not just of programmatic, but also of fiscal, relief. The upshot has been a marked escalation of state and local government challenges to the property and income tax exemptions that nonprofit organizations have long enjoyed at the local level.[51]

- Health organizations, perhaps the most exposed part of the nonprofit sector because of their scale and commercial prowess, were among the first to feel the effects of this sentiment.[52] Nonprofit Health Maintenance Organizations faced threats to their tax-exempt status early on, and this proved to be one of the factors leading most of them to convert to the for-profit form over the past 20 years. Blue Cross health insurance organizations lost most of their federal tax benefits in the 1986 Tax Reform Act, and many of them are now following the HMOs into the for-profit world. Now assaults are being mounted against the tax exemptions of hospitals. Such challenges were "unheard of in decades past,"[53] yet they have recently surfaced in more than 20 states.

- In the course of challenging the tax exemptions of hospitals, states are establishing legal precedents that could have far wider implications. Recent state supreme court decisions in Utah and Pennsylvania, for example, have explicitly rejected the prevailing Federal common law concept of "charity" so far as hospitals are concerned. Under this common law precept, the promotion of health is considered to be an inherently charitable activity. Nonprofit hospitals thus qualify for charitable status even if their patients pay for their care so long as the institutions use all profits for " 'the maintenance or improvement of the institution or some other charitable purpose.' "[54] Instead of this standard, the Utah Supreme Court established a *quid pro quo* test under which a hospital can lose its exemption from state and local property taxes unless it meets three conditions: (a) it is supported mainly by donations and gifts, (b) most of its patients receive their care for free or reduced cost, and (c) income is sufficient only to cover operating and long-term maintenance costs.[55] Using this standard, most nonprofit hospitals involved in the Medicare program would likely be vulnerable to a loss of-tax exempt status.

- This same logic has now been applied in Pennsylvania not only to hospitals, but also to institutions of higher education, despite the fact that education is explicitly identified in the most authoritative summary of the English common law concept of charity as an inherently "charitable" purpose.[56]

- What is more, the scope of such challenges appears to be widening. Using a combination of three principal arguments— (a) that local tax exemptions should be available only to organizations that primarily serve the poor; (b) that all "commercial income," including that from fees and charges, as well as the property used to produce it, should be taxed; and (c) that local tax exemptions should be limited to organizations that primarily serve people who live in the same town or state,[57] assessors in a wide assortment of states have launched challenges against local nonprofit institutions. A recent study found, for example, that at least two-thirds of Pennsylvania counties are actively seeking taxes—or payments in lieu of taxes—from nonprofits, and such challenges are widespread as well in New York, New Hampshire, Oregon, Maine, and Wisconsin. A recent ballot initiative in Colorado would have denied tax exemption to all but a handful of charitable institutions, including all churches. Although this provision was roundly defeated, opponents fear that a revised version, preserving the exemption for churches, could ultimately win broader support.

- Many of these same issues are now surfacing at the federal level as well. Thus, as noted earlier, the so-called "commerciality" test has been built into the proposed national sales tax, so that nonprofits providing services that are "commercially available" would be subject to tax on these sales. Despite the ambiguity of the concept of "commercially available," efforts are under way to introduce this concept into the existing income tax system as a substitute for the existing "relatedness" test.

## Zoning Restrictions

Nonprofit organizations are also being targeted increasingly in NMBY (Not in My Backyard) regulations at the local level. The Hartford City Council, for example, approved an ordinance in November 1995 establishing a moratorium on all new homeless shelters, rehabilitation homes, and other treatment or social service centers in the city. A recent study revealed that at least 30 cities have similar statutes or regulations that employ zoning or building codes to exclude service agencies.[58]

## Anti-Advocacy Legislation

Finally, the so-called Istook Amendment at the Federal level (and counterpart legislation at the state level) has brought the same kind of challenge to one of the other fundamental functions of the voluntary sector—namely, its advocacy and representational function. Under this amendment, which came close to passage in the 104th Congress, nonprofit organizations receiving federal grants would be severely limited in using even their private revenues to engage in a broad range of advocacy and representational activities. This would undercut one of the major rationales for the existence of a nonprofit sector—that is, to give voice to the underrepresented and to bring new issues to public attention. That this provision made the headway it did is testimony to the vulnerability of the nonprofit sector at the present time. Having joined with government to respond to public needs, nonprofit organizations are now in the uncomfortable position of appearing to be advocating not on behalf of the clients and communities they serve, but in their own self interest, for the budgets and programs that support their own operations. This has opened them to the kind of attack recently leveled by Heritage Foundation President Edwin Feulner, who has sought to discredit nonprofit support for expanded public benefits to the poor on grounds that the agencies advancing these claims are themselves "on the public take" and therefore advocating not for their clientele but for their own organizational budgets. It is this vulnerability that proposals of the sort embodied in the Istook Amendment seek to exploit.

## Summary

In short, a significant challenge confronts the American nonprofit sector at the present time. This challenge is part fiscal, part economic, part political, and part philosophical and moral. Nonprofit organizations are being forced or enticed into modes of behavior that diverge increasingly sharply from public expectations and norms, and too little is being done to bring either the reality back into alignment with expectations, or expectations into better alignment with reality. The upshot is a dangerous crisis of confidence and legitimacy for one of the oldest, most venerated, and most critical components of our national heritage.

# CHAPTER 3

# Countervailing Trends

Before deciding what, if anything, should be done about the set of
challenges outlined above, we need to acknowledge two further
points. The first is that similar challenges have confronted the
nonprofit sector in the past, yet the sector has survived. After all, the
current American infatuation with nonprofit organizations was far
from politically correct in the early years of the Republic, and
defenders of the sector have perceived damaging challenges from
more recent developments as well, such as the emergence of federal
involvement in the social welfare field during the New Deal and
the assault on foundations embodied in the Tax Reform Act of
1969. In each case, however, the sector survived and prospered,
though often in changed form.

What is more, while critical challenges confront the American
nonprofit sector at the present time, a number of countervailing
trends are also in evidence. Three of these in particular deserve
mention here.

### Continued Grass-roots Energies

Perhaps most heartening is the recent evidence of continued vitality
in the grass-roots base of the nonprofit sector throughout the
country. While established nonprofit organizations may have grown
more bureaucratic and distant from the problems they are supposed
to address, new organizations seem to be taking their place, renew-
ing the sector and reconnecting it to its fundamental purposes.
Indeed, journalist Robin Garr has perceived a widespread process of
community reinvention underway across the country. Responding

to the twin challenges of federal budget cuts and economic recession in the early 1980s, a wide assortment of emergency feeding programs, temporary housing facilities, AIDS clinics, and self-help groups of various sorts popped up in communities across the land. As problems persisted, moreover, emergency facilities evolved into congregate shelters, soup kitchens, food banks, and, ultimately, "multiple-purpose organizations that didn't just feed the hungry and homeless people, but sought to identify their problems and do whatever was needed to move them back into the mainstream." As Garr points out, "[t]hese initiatives did not trickle down from the federal government, or from foundations, or from think tanks or academe. They rose *up* from the grass roots. They developed out of the common-sense ideas of foot soldiers in the war on poverty, drawing on good old-fashioned know-how, creativity, and American can-do spirit."[59]

Not only the needs of the poor, but other needs as well have recently been the focus of grass-roots civic action. Despite recent concerns about the deterioration of the civic infrastructure of American communities,[60] in fact there is striking evidence of a civic revival in the United States, or at least of continued civic vitality. Data assembled by Sydney Verba at Harvard, for example, reveal that as of the early 1990s almost 80 percent of Americans reported an affiliation with at least one association. This included 44 percent who were affiliated with a charitable or social service organization, 25 percent with an education organization, 23 percent with a business or professional association, and 21 percent with a hobby, sports, or leisure association.[61] While labor union participation may have declined, new social movements have emerged to take labor's place as vehicles for recruiting new participants into civic life. The environmental movement, for example, has experienced a massive upsurge in recent years. Nor is this merely the "paper" membership sometimes assumed. Rather, a vibrant grass-roots culture has emerged involving hundreds of thousands of people. "On almost a daily basis," reports one account, "a plethora of meetings, social gatherings, hikes, bike trips, clean-up projects, rallies, nature workshops, and the like are held in communities across the nation by local chapters of national environmental organizations, as well as ad-hoc community groups."[62] As the title of a recent review article puts it, "The Data Just Don't Show Erosion of America's 'Social Capital.' "[63] Evidently, the wellsprings of voluntary action continue to percolate in contemporary American society.

## Intergenerational Transfer of Wealth

A second potentially promising development for the nonprofit sector is the intergenerational transfer of wealth that is anticipated over the next forty years between the Depression-era generation and the postwar baby boomers. According to an influential 1993 study by economists Robert Avery and Michael Rendell of Cornell University, an extraordinary $10 trillion dollars will be transferred in this process. This wealth accumulated in the hands of the Depression era generation as a consequence of their relatively high propensity to save; their fortuitous investment during the 1950s and 1960s in relatively low-cost houses that then escalated in value during the real estate boom of the 1970s; and the stock market surge of the 1980s and 1990s, which substantially boosted the value of their investments.[64] Also contributing to the potential wealth available for transfer have been powerful economic trends and policies that have substantially increased income levels at the upper end of the economic scale, accentuating inequalities but leaving substantial sums of money in the hands of fewer people. Between 1979 and 1989, for example, the share of the nation's wealth controlled by the top 1 percent of households climbed from 20 percent to almost 40 percent.[65] Indeed, one third of the projected intergenerational transfer is expected to go to 1 percent of the boomer generation, for an average inheritance of $1.6 million among this select few.

With so much money "in play," substantial opportunities exist for the expansion of charitable bequests. The experience of the 1980s is certainly encouraging in this respect. During that decade alone, about a third of all foundations now in existence were formed, including 3,000 with assets of at least $1 million.[66]

The problem, however, is that this is not the only potential use of these inheritances, and investment managers have been hard at work devising more profitable alternatives. What is more, the projected inheritances may never materialize, or never materialize to the extent anticipated, if life expectancy continues to expand and medical or nursing-care costs absorb more than the anticipated share of the accumulation. To take advantage of the opportunities that may exist, charitable institutions and the fundraising community have therefore had to begin mobilizing their energies. Community foundations have been particularly aggressive in reaching out to wealthy individuals, but other charities are increasingly involved as well.[67] The prospect of significant intergenerational transfers has also helped spawn a major new charitable industry as investment houses have moved actively into the "charity business" to establish charitable gift funds through which wealthy individuals can manage their charitable contributions side-by-side with the management of their investments. Such funds avoid the complications of setting up a foundation, yet have many of the advantages of a community foundation in permitting a donor to reap the full tax benefit of contributing an appreciated property at its current fair market value rather than at its purchase price. Though only a few years old, such funds already rival community foundations in the scale of their recent growth.[68]

Although it is far from clear what the real benefit to charitable institutions will be from the intergenerational transfer that is anticipated, the possibility alone seems likely to offer encouragement of a sort, and such encouragement is highly welcome by hard-pressed charitable institutions.

### A New Paradigm for Corporate Philanthropy

A third potentially important development in the world of nonprofit action is the reorientation of corporate philanthropy that has been under way for the past several years. While corporate giving has proved far more disappointing than many had hoped in the early 1980s, a new mode of corporate involvement in community affairs has been slowly taking its place. Central to this new mode is the integration of corporate social responsibility activities more firmly into the strategic operations of companies in ways that enhance the companies' self-interest while promoting socially useful causes, frequently in strategic alliance with nonprofit organizations. Such collaborations have also been justified as a way to foster greater employee loyalty and morale, and thus to promote the "total quality" commitment that firms have increasingly adopted. As described by one of its most ardent students, corporations adopting this approach "hunt for a reconciliation of their companies' profit-making strategies with the welfare of society, and they search for ways to steer all parts of the company on a socially engaged course."[69]

The great virtue of this approach is that it makes corporate managers available to nonprofit organizations not simply as donors, but also as allies and collaborators in a wide range of socially important missions. While there are admittedly dangers of exploiting the good name of the nonprofit organization to promote the narrow commercial objectives of the company, there are also intriguing possibilities for extremely productive partnerships that could pay off handsomely for the nonprofit organizations and those they serve.

## Conclusion and Implications

In short, despite the significant challenges the nonprofit sector faces at the present time, there are also a number of countervailing trends that provide some basis for hope. Whether the positive trends will prove sufficient to offset the more troubling ones, however, is more difficult to say. Despite significant evidence indicating continued revitalization of the organizational base of the sector, for example, new organizations eventually come up against the same hard realities of institutional survival that confront many of the existing agencies. One of the central conclusions of journalist Robin Garr's journey among *The Grassroots Movements that are Feeding the Hungry, Housing the Homeless, and Putting Americans Back to Work*, for example, is that splendid isolation is not a tenable posture for even these grass-roots initiatives. "Nonprofits have demonstrated a consistent ability to understand local problems and overcome them with creative, flexible approaches," he concludes. "But they rarely have sufficient resources." What is needed, therefore, is to "take fullest advantage of every opportunity to build partnerships between government and the nonprofit groups...."[70] The ultimate success and staying power of many of the new citizen initiatives therefore turn out to depend heavily on precisely the same government fiscal policies that are affecting the existing agencies as well.

While the prospect of significant intergenerational wealth transfer and a changing corporate posture toward the voluntary sector offer much-needed relief, moreover, the extent of this relief is open to serious question. As we have seen, the recent record of bequest giving is hardly encouraging. Far from increasing, the relative scale of bequest giving has been on the decline. While some boost in private charitable giving seems likely, the scale hardly compares with the anticipated reductions in public support. Similarly, the reorientation of corporate philanthropy has recently come up against the hard realities of corporate downsizing. In re-engineering the corporation, many corporate managements are re-engineering the corporate philanthropy activity out of existence. Under the circumstances, the pressures on the nation's nonprofit sector are likely to persist.

# CHAPTER 4

# Next Steps: The Search for Renewal

The American nonprofit sector thus appears to be at another critical turning point in its history. Although ambivalence, not unvarnished affection, has been the prevailing attitude toward nonprofit institutions throughout most of American history, that ambivalence has taken a special edge in recent years. Never fully comfortable with the idea of private institutions controlling large amounts of wealth, Americans ultimately made peace with the nonprofit sector as a way to indulge their preferences for individualism, for self-expression, for the exercise of personal initiative, and for private over public action to pursue even public ends. The implicit understanding, however, was that the resulting set of institutions would remain largely volunteer-based, separate from government, and dedicated to those most in need. This, at any rate, was the image of the nonprofit sector that has come down to us in national mythology and that has been sustained by powerful political ideologies.

Now that it is becoming clear that significant parts of the nonprofit sector diverge rather sharply from that quaint nineteenth-century ideal, critical questions are being raised about the future of this set of institutions. How to respond to these questions has consequently become quite a matter of concern.

For some, the appropriate response is denial or acquiescence in the changes under way. Those adhering to this point of view accept the drift toward commercialization as a reasonable response to the pressures the nonprofit sector is under and discount the seriousness of the challenges the sector is facing. According to this perspective, the nonprofit sector has experienced previous challenges and nevertheless managed to survive. Overreacting to the current developments could therefore cause more problems than it solves, particularly since these developments hardly affect all portions of the sector equally. Why put the entire sector at risk, therefore, because of difficulties facing only a portion? Better just to lie low and wait out the storm.

A second approach endorses the current critique of the non-profit sector and urges radical changes to bring the sector back to its presumed historical roots. Those who advocate this approach feel that the current assault on the nonprofit sector, like the one in the early 1980s, is at least partly warranted:

- That nonprofit organizations have grown far too dependent on government;

- That principal reliance should be placed on the sector's private charitable and volunteer base;

- That the sector is too heavily involved in advocacy and should focus its energies instead on service delivery for those in need; and

- That nonprofits have no business getting involved in commercial activities, including fee-based service delivery, that might interfere with private businesses.

By cutting back on government support, restricting commercial income, and limiting advocacy, this argument goes, the nonprofit sector would be forced to return to its traditional mission, would become more efficient, and would reconnect to the constituencies it is supposed to serve.

While each of these two responses has merit, it is the argument here that neither is ultimately acceptable, that the problems facing the nonprofit sector are sufficiently momentous to warrant more than the patronizing "been there/seen that" response of the denial and accommodation school, but that the "golden era" of nonprofit independence evoked by those proposing a return to the past never really existed and would be counterproductive for our own day even if it had. A third route therefore seems advisable.

The inspiration for such a third route can be found in the work of John Gardner, a long-standing advocate of the nonprofit sector. In his book, *Self-Renewal*, Gardner argues that "Unless we attend to the requirements of renewal, aging institutions and organizations will eventually bring our civilization to moldering ruin."

I believe that Gardner's admonition about the need for continuous self-renewal applies forcefully to the circumstances of the nonprofit sector at the present time; we should respond to the challenges the nonprofit sector is facing not with a vain attempt to return to a mythical golden age of supposed nonprofit purity, nor a policy of continued drift toward greater commercialization, but by using this as an occasion, and an opportunity, for renewal. This would entail rethinking the nonprofit sector's role and operations, re-examining the prevailing mythology in the light of contemporary realities, and seeking a new consensus, a new settlement, regarding the functions of nonprofit organizations, the relationships they have with citizens, with government, and with business, and the way they will operate in the years ahead.

Central to such an approach is acceptance of the validity of what might be termed the "partnership model" of nonprofit operations, the view that nonprofit organizations cannot effectively operate in splendid isolation, that they can preserve their distinctive character and role while working collaboratively with government and the business sector to address pressing public problems. Such an approach relies on nonprofits for what they do best—identifying problems, mobilizing fresh thinking and energy, caring for those in need on a human scale, and promoting social change—while enlisting the other sectors for what they do best—generating resources, establishing societal priorities, and guaranteeing rights in the case of government; and providing legitimacy, expertise, and assistance in the case of business. The challenge of renewal is therefore to find ways to protect and enhance what is unique and special about nonprofit organizations while accepting the reality, and the advantages, of partnerships between nonprofit organizations and the other components of American life. The challenge, in short, is to forge a true "civil society," i.e., a society that contains three distinct sectors—government, business, and not-for-profit—but that fosters active cooperation among them in addressing societal needs.[71]

What might such a strategy of renewal involve? Broadly speaking, a number of steps seem essential.

## Values and Futures

First and foremost, renewal requires a reexamination of basic values and beliefs. As Gardner puts it:

> Anyone concerned about the continuous renewal of society must be concerned for the renewal of that society's values and beliefs. Societies are renewed—if they are renewed at all—by people who believe in something, care about something, stand for something.[72]

The evolution of the nonprofit sector in this country has clearly leaped beyond what our existing concepts and values are able to accommodate very easily.

- Traditional concepts of charity and altruism, of care for the less fortunate, now sit uneasily with the reality of large-scale charitable enterprises which are headed by well-paid professionals and provide assistance to far more than those in greatest financial need.

- The religious taproots of the charitable sector, with their emphasis on sacrifice and duty, must now make room for new impulses stressing empowerment, self-realization, self-help, and even self-interest.

- A sector whose mythology celebrates independence must now come to terms with the need for close working relationships with business and government to solve pressing problems.

- Traditional notions of arms-length philanthropy, alms-giving, and service as the principal vehicles of nonprofit action must now come to terms with new demands for citizen involvement, for active engagement in societal problem-solving, and even for direct means of deciding which public goods are worthy of support. This may require not only new ways of thinking, but also new legal structures.

## Concrete Actions

To give focus to this process of re-thinking, a number of concrete action steps will need to be seriously explored. Among the steps that merit such scrutiny are these:

- Replacement of the current tax deduction system, in whole or in part, with a system of tax credits for charitable contributions, especially for non-itemizers. Such a move, if carefully structured, could provide a potent stimulus to private giving.

- Deregulation of nonprofit advocacy to ensure that nonprofits can respond to the new citizen demands for involvement that now exist, and that *should* exist, in a robust democracy.

- Establishment of a Charity Bank or other forms of credit mechanisms to provide risk capital to nonprofit agencies and thus better enable these agencies to compete with for-profit firms and remain on the cutting edge of technology.

- Identification or development of new models of partnership that can more effectively connect the nonprofit sector with government and business;

- Establishment of guidelines to reconcile the growth of fee-for-service revenue with the charitable functions of the nonprofit sector and with popular conceptions of the sector's mission and responsibilities.

- Creation of a Charity Credit Card to facilitate contributions to the public good just the way commercial credit cards facilitate contributions to the private good of purchasers.

- Adoption of a *Good Housekeeping Seal of Approval*-type mechanism for corporations that make concerted efforts to engage actively in civic life not simply through charitable contributions, but also through direct involvement with government and nonprofit organizations.

• Increased use of *matching grants* by government to tie public funding more directly to citizen desires and provide incentives for nonprofit organizations to preserve their volunteer and charitable bases of support.

• Reexamination of the tax exemption system to determine if some part of the exemption should be based on the nature of the *activities* an organization undertakes, rather than the nature of the *organization*. This would essentially extend the concept of the Unrelated Business Income Tax to a larger portion of nonprofit operations.

### Civil Society Commissions

Proposals such as this, and the values that lie behind them, not only need to be carefully analyzed. They also need to be subjected to public review. To engage a broader public in this dialogue, a network of state-level Civil Society Commissions could usefully be organized throughout the United States. The purpose of such commissions would be to address the critical issues facing the nonprofit sector, to examine some of the steps that might be taken to keep this sector vital, and to articulate a new consensus, a new social compact, about the role this sector should play, in concert with business and government, in solving our public problems.

The "infrastructure" organizations that now serve the nonprofit sector at the local level—the state associations of nonprofit organizations and the regional associations of grantmakers—could play a pivotal role in such a process along with other leading nonprofit and philanthropic institutions at both the national and local levels. The resulting commissions could take an important step toward articulating new models of collaboration and a new understanding about how to mobilize and blend the energies of all three sectors— business, government, and nonprofit—in improving the quality of American life.

## Public Education

Finally, a serious media campaign is needed to educate the public at large about the nonprofit sector and the role it plays. What is needed, however, is not a media campaign that deals in mythology. It should not portray the nonprofit sector operating in splendid isolation and supported only by private giving to solve our nation's problems. That is no longer the reality of contemporary social problem-solving, if indeed it ever was. What should be emphasized instead is the modern reality of nonprofit organizations working collaboratively with government and the business sector to mobilize public energies and respond to societal needs. This may be a complex message, but it is the reality that now prevails and the one that holds the greatest promise for the future. Yet it is a reality that has unfortunately been invisible in the public mind.

# Conclusion

Alexis de Tocqueville, who understood more clearly than most the vital contribution that nonprofit associations make to American society, also understood the great obstacles they face. "Unhappily," de Tocqueville noted, "the same social condition that renders associations so necessary to democratic nations [i.e.,equality of condition] renders their formation more difficult among those nations than among all others."

For our own time, we might add that this condition also renders the survival of these organizations problematic as well. At the very least, it should be clear from the discussion here that America's nonprofit sector is experiencing significant strains at the present time—strains that result at least in part from lack of understanding about the role that this set of organizations should appropriately play in an advanced industrial society that has recognized, however begrudgingly, the need for a significant governmental role in public problem-solving as well. To be sure, these strains are far from universal. Nor are they wholly negative in their implications. Yet there is reason for serious concern about the battering that significant elements of this sector have been experiencing, and about the directions many organizations have been forced to take as a consequence. While there is doubtless enough resilience in the nation's nonprofit sector to survive these pressures, a more sensible course might still be to take stock of what is happening and decide what can be done to minimize the damage and chart a more defensible course for the future. It is just such a reassessment and redirection that this report suggests is long past due.

# Notes

1. Waldemar Nielsen, *The Endangered Sector* (New York: Columbia University, 1979), p. 33.

2. Peter Dobkin Hall, "A Historical Overview of the Private Nonprofit Sector," in Walter Powell, *The Nonprofit Sector: A Research Handbook* (New Haven: Yale University Press, 1987), pp. 4–5.

3. See, for example: Lester M. Salamon, *America's Nonprofit Sector: A Primer* (New York: Foundation Center, 1992); Michael O'Neill, *The Third America* (San Francisco: Jossey-Bass Publishers, 1989); Waldemar Nielsen, *The Endangered Sector* (New York: Columbia University Press, 1979).

4. The 1.3 million figure is estimated by adding to the 1.1 million organizations registered with the Internal Revenue Service approximately 200,000 of the 341,000 U.S. churches that we assume are not registered with the IRS, since this is not required under the First Amendment's prohibition on established religion. The estimate of nonprofit sector operating expenditures is from Virginia Hodgkinson, Murray S. Weitzman, et. al., *Nonprofit Almanac, 1996-1997: Dimensions of the Independent Sector* (San Francisco: Jossey-Bass Publishers, 1996), p. 46.

5. See, for example: James S. Coleman, *Foundations of Social Theory* (Cambridge, Mass: Harvard University Press, 1990), pp. 300–321; Robert Putnam, *Making Democracy Work: Civic Traditions in Modern Italy* (Princeton: Princeton University Press, 1993), pp. 83–116, 163–185.

6. Alexis de Tocqueville, *Democracy in America*. The Henry Reeve Text (New York: Vintage Books, 1945), Vol. 2, p. 117.

7. This development and its resulting scope and structure are explored more fully in: Lester M. Salamon, *Partners in Public Service: Government-Nonprofit Relations in the Modern Welfare State*, (Baltimore: Johns Hopkins University Press, 1995).

8. Waldemar Nielsen, *The Endangered Sector* (New York: Columbia University Press, 1979), p. 27.

9. John S. Whitehead, *The Separation of College and State: Columbia, Dartmouth, Harvard, and Yale, 1776-1876* (New Haven: Yale University Press, 1973).

10. Marvin Olsasky, *The Tragedy of American Compassion* (Washington, D.C.: Regnery Publishing, Inc., 1992).

11. Robert Bremner, *The Public Good: Philanthropy and Welfare in the Civil War Era* (New York: Alfred A. Knopf, 1980), p. 162.

12. Frank Fetter, "The Subsidizing of Private Charities," *Journal of Sociology*, (1901/02), pp. 359–85.

13. Patrick Riley, "Family Services," in N. Gilbert and H. Sprecht, *Handbook of the Social Services* (Englewood Cliffs, NJ: Prentice-Hall, 1981), p. 90; Peter Goldberg, "The State of the American Nonprofit Sector," unpublished paper (September 1996).

14. Based on data from *Giving USA: 1996* (New York: AAFRC Trust for Philanthropy, 1996), p. 15.

15. Salamon, *Partners in Public Service*, p. 186.

16. Most federal programs are "discretionary programs" that receive their funding through annual appropriations bills passed by the Congress and approved by the President. Included here are programs such as Head Start, Community Development Block Grants (CDBG), Social Service Block Grants, job training. However, most federal domestic spending flows through so-called "entitlement programs," which do not require annual appropriations. Rather, spending levels in these programs are determined by the authorizing legislation for the programs, which sets eligibility standards for receipt of benefits. Anybody meeting these standards is automatically "entitled" to the benefits so that the spending levels are determined by the number of people eligible and the share of these who show up

and demand the benefits.

Prior to 1984, Congress had no mechanism for considering spending levels for both the discretionary and the entitlement programs together. Beginning that year, however, Congress established a budget process that requires the passage of an initial Budget Resolution in the spring and a final Budget Resolution in the Fall addressing both sets of programs. Under Congressional procedures, appropriations committees and legislative authorizing committees are then obliged to meet the targets set in the Budget Resolution for their respective sets of programs. If they do not, Congress can pass a "Reconciliation Bill" that incorporates the necessary changes in both appropriations and entitlement program benefit and eligibility levels.

The budget resolutions apply to Congressional action only and do not require presidential approval. Reconciliation bills, however, must be approved by the President to become law, unless they are passed over his veto.

17. Under the welfare reform bill, the federal government's automatic guarantee to match state payments to eligible fatherless families with dependent children was ended and replaced with a fixed grant to states. In addition, this grant was conditioned on state termination of assistance to families which had received these benefits for more than five years and assistance to immigrants was restricted.

18. Thus, compared to a Congressional Budget Office projection of $144 billion for fiscal year 1996, the actual deficit has turned out to be $107 billion, the lowest in real dollar terms since 1979. The major reason for this appears to be higher-than-expected increases in federal revenue collections spurred in part by economic growth. Congressional Budget Office, "The Economic and Budget Outlook: FY 1997-2006," May 1996.

19. Computed from data in Virginia Ann Hodgkinson and Murray S. Weitzman with John Abrahams, Eric Crutchfield, and David R. Stevenson, *Nonprofit Almanac, 1996-1997: Dimensions of the Independent Sector* (San Francisco: Jossey-Bass Publishers, 1996), p. 81. [Cited hereafter as Hodgkinson and Weitzman, *Nonprofit Almanac.*]

20. Internal Revenue Service, *Statistics of Income Bulletin,* various editions, as reported in Hodgkinson and Weitzman, *Nonprofit Almanac,* 1996, p. 89.

21. Internal Revenue Service, *Statistics of Income Bulletin,* Individual Income Tax Returns, as reported in *Nonprofit Almanac* (1996), Table 2.4, p. 91.

22. Based on data in Barry W. Johnson, "Estate Tax Returns," *Statistics of Income,* various years, as reported in Independent Sector, *Nonprofit Almanac,* 1996, Table 2.7, p. 91.

23. Julian Wolpert, *Patterns of Generosity in America: Who's Holding the Safety Net* (New York: Twentieth Century Fund, 1993), p. 40.

24. Charles T. Clotfelter and Richard Schmalbeck, "The Impact of Fundamental Tax Reform on Nonprofit Organizations," in Henry J. Aaron and William G. Gale, eds., *Economic Effects of Fundamental Tax Reform* (Washington, D.C.: The Brookings Institution, 1996), pp. 211-243.

25. The one compensating feature of this proposal is that to remain "revenue neutral" it would have to impose fairly high marginal tax rates on middle-income taxpayers, lowering their cost of giving, and potentially boosting their giving.

26. The discussion here draws on: Council on Foundations/Independent Sector, Working Group on Tax Restructuring. "Impact of Tax Restructuring Proposals on Charitable Entities," mimeo, September 1996.

27. Lester M. Salamon, "The Marketization of Welfare: Changing Nonprofit and For-Profit Roles in the American Welfare State," *Social Service Review,* Vol 67, No. 1 (March 1993), pp. 16-39.

28. See, for example: Harris Meyer,

Terese Hudson, James E. Cain, Stewart L. Carr, and David Zacharias, "Selling... or Selling Out," *Hospitals and Health Networks* (June 5, 1996), p. 22; Montague Brown, "Commentary: The Commercialization of America's Voluntary Health Care System," *Health Care Management Review* (1996), 21 (3), pp. 13-18; Malik Hasan, "Let's End the Nonprofit Charade," *New England Journal of Medicine* (April 18, 1996), Vol 334, No. 16, pp. 1055-8; Anne Lowrey Bailey, "Health Care's Merger Mania," *Chronicle of Philanthropy* (November 16, 1995), p. 1.

29. See, for example: Milt Freudenheim, "Health Plans in New Jersey Face Rivalries," *New York Times* (May 30, 1996); Milt Freudenheim, "For Blue Cross, at Crossroads, A Fight to Save Role for System," *New York Times* (June 15, 1996); Milt Freudenheim, "Empire Blue Cross Seeks Permission to Earn Profits," *New York Times* (September 26, 1996).

30. "Health Care," *Chicago Tribune* (April 14, 1996).

31. Dr. Malik Hasan, "Let's End the Nonprofit Charade," *New England Journal of Medicine* (April 18, 1996), Vol 334, No. 16, pp. 1055-8.

32. Nina Bernstein, "Giant Companies Entering Race to Run State Welfare Programs," *The New York Times* (September 15, 1996), p. A1.

33. One source puts the value of clinical practice fees at 40 percent of the income at medical schools nationwide. William Richardson, "The Appropriate Scale of the Health Sciences Enterprise," *Daedalus* (Fall 1993), p. 186.

34. Jonathan R. Cole, "Balancing Acts: Dilemmas of Choice Facing Research Universities," *Daedalus* (Fall 1993), p. 31.

35. Lisbeth Schorr, *Within Our Reach: Breaking the Cycle of Disadvantage* (New York: Anchor books, 1988).

36. Kimberly Dennis, "Charities on the Dole," *Policy Review: The Journal of American Citizenship*, No. 76 (March-April 1996).

37. See, for example: Marvin Olasky, *The Tragedy of American Compassion* (Washington, D.C.: Regnery Publishing, Inc., 1992).

38. Roy Lubove, *The Professional Altruist* (Cambridge: Harvard University Pres, 1965), p. 23.

39. Lubove, *Professional Altruist*, p. 220.

40. H. Hasenfeld and English, *Human Service Organizations* (Englewood Cliffs: Prentice Hall, 1974), p. 19.

41. David Rosner, *A Once Charitable Enterprise: Hospitals and Health Care in Brooklyn and New York, 1885-1915* (Princeton: Princeton University Press, 1982), p. 6.

42. John McKnight, *The Careless Society: Community and its Counterfeits* (New York: Basic Books, 1995), p. 10.

43. Stuart Butler, *Privatizing Federal Spending* (New York: Universe Books, 1985).

44. See, for example: Martin Anderson, *Imposters in the Temple: American Intellectuals are Destroying Our Universities and Cheating our Students* (Englewood Cliffs, N.J.: Simon and Schuster, 1992).

45. This line of argument is developed most forcefully in Henry Hansman, "The Role of Nonprofit Enterprise," *Yale Law Journal* 89 (1980), pp. 835-901.

46. Regina Herzlinger, "Can Public Trust in Nonprofits and Governments be Restored?" *Harvard Business Review* (March-April 1996), p. 98.

47. See, for example, the special issue on "accountability of nonprofit organizations" in *Nonprofit Management and Leadership*, Volume 6, No. 2 (Winter 1995), pp. 121-196.

48. Data on popular confidence in nonprofit organizations exclusive of education and religion, and in small business and the military from: Virginia Hodgkinson and Murray Weizman, *Giving and Volunteering in the United States, 1994* edition. (Washington: Independent Sector, 1994). Data on popular confidence in state and federal governments for 1995

and 1975 from: Hart/Teeter, "A National Public Opinion Survey Conducted for the Council for Excellence in Government," March 1995, p. 4.

49. Capital Research Center, "Our Mission," Capital Research Center World Wide Web Site (November 1996).

50. See, for example: Edwin Feulner, "Truth in Testimony," *Heritage Foundation Testimony* (August 22, 1996).

51. Historically, state and local governments have extended property and income tax exemptions to organizations that qualify for tax exemption under federal income tax rules. However, the state treatment of the tax status of nonprofit organizations is completely independent of the treatment these organizations receive under federal law. States are therefore free to tax or not tax organizations that are exempt from federal income taxation, so long as they otherwise do not infringe on federal constitutional prohibitions against interfering with interstate commerce and denial of "equal protection of the laws."

52. The material here draws heavily on: Bradford H. Gray, "Challenges Facing Nonprofit Health Care Organizations," unpublished memorandum (September 1996), p. 6.

53. Margaret A. Potter and Beaufort B. Longest, Jr., "The Divergence of Federal and State Policies on the Charitable Tax Exemption of Nonprofit Hospitals," *Journal of Health Politics, Policy, and Law,* Vol. 19, No. 2 (Summer 1994), p. 394.

54. American Law Institute, *Restatement of the Law of Trusts 2d* (1959), quoted in Potter and Longest, "Divergence," p. 397.

55. *Utah County v. Intermountain Health Care* 709 P. 2d 265 (Utah 1985), cited in Potter and Longest, (1994), p. 411.

56. In *Pemsel's case* (1891), British Lord MacNaghten provided what has come to be the definitive summary of the meaning of the term "charitable" in the British common law tradition by identifying

"four principal divisions"—i.e., relief of poverty, advancement of education, advancement of religion, and "other purposes beneficial to the community..."

57. *State Tax Trends for Nonprofits,* Vol 4, No. 2 (Spring 1996), p. 9.

58. Jonathan Rabinovitz, "Fighting Poverty Programs," *New York Times* (March 24, 1996).

59. Robin Garr, *Reinvesting in America: The Grassroots Movements that are Feeding the Hungry, Housing the Homeless, and Putting Americans Back to Work* (Reading, MA: Addison-Wesley Publishing Company, 1995).

60. See, for example, Robert Putnam, "Bowling Alone: America's Declining Social Capital," *The Journal of Democracy* (Winter 1995).

61. Sydney Verba et. al., *Voice and Equality: Civic Voluntarism in American Politics* (Cambridge, MA: Harvard University Press, 1995), pp. 58-65.

62. George Pettinico, "Civic Participation Alive and Well in Today's Environmental Groups," *The Public Perspective* (June/July 1996).

63. Everett C. Ladd. "The Data Just Don't Show Erosion of America's Social Capital," *The Public Perspective* (June/July 1996), p. 1.

64. For a summary of the current thinking on this intergenerational wealth transfer, see: Harvey D. Shapiro, "The Coming Inheritance Bonanza," *Institutional Investor,* Vol XXXVIII, No. 6 (June 1994), pp. 143-148.

65. Edward N. Wolf, *Top Heavy: The Increasing Inequality of Wealth in America and What Can Be Done About It,* An Expanded Edition of a Twentieth Century Fund Report (New York: The New Press, 1996), pp. 7-8.

66. Loren Renz, *Foundation Giving, 1995.* (New York: The Foundation Center, 1995), p. 3.

67. See, for example: "A Generation Prepares to Transfer Its Trillions," *The Chronicle of Philanthropy,* Vol Vi, No. 3

(November 16, 1993), pp. 1, 10-12.

68. Fidelity Investment's Charitable Gift Fund received $186 billion in contributions in 1995, making it the twenty-second largest charity in the country in terms of donations received. Stephen G. Greene, "Financial Titans' Move into Charity," *The Chronicle of Philanthropy,* Vol. IX, No. 4 (November 28, 1996), pp. 1, 26.

69. Craig Smith, "The New Corporate Philanthropy," *Harvard Business Review* (May/June 1994), p. 107.

70. Garr, *Reinvesting,* pp.231-232.

71. For further elaboration of this concept of "civil society," see: Lester M. Salamon and Helmut K. Anheier, "The Civil Society Sector," *Society* (January/February 1997), pp. 60-65.

72. John Gardner, *Self-Renewal: The Individual and the Innovative Society,* Revised edition (New York: W. W. Norton & Co., 1981), p. 115.

## About the Author

LESTER M. SALAMON is a professor at The Johns Hopkins University and director of the Johns Hopkins Institute for Policy Studies. Dr. Salamon is one of the pioneers in the empirical study of the nonprofit sector in the United States and around the world. His book, *America's Nonprofit Sector: A Primer* (New York: The Foundation Center, 1992), is a standard text in courses on the nonprofit sector throughout the United States. His monograph, *The Emerging Nonprofit Sector* (Manchester, U. K.: Manchester University Press, 1996), is the first effort to document the scope, scale, structure, and role of the nonprofit sector at the international level using a systematic comparative approach. And his recent book, *Partners in Public Service: Government-Nonprofit Relations in the Modern Welfare State* (Baltimore: Johns Hopkins University Press, 1995), won the 1996 Distinguished Book Award of the Association for Research on Nonprofit Organizations and Voluntary Action (ARNOVA). Dr. Salamon received his B.A. in economics and policy studies from Princeton University and his Ph.D. in government from Harvard University. He has taught at Vanderbilt, Duke, and Tougaloo College and served as Deputy Associate Director of the U.S. Office of Management and Budget.